# Fearless

# Louise Minchin

# Fearless

## Adventures with extraordinary women

BLOOMSBURY SPORT

LONDON · OXFORD · NEW YORK · NEW DELHI · SYDNEY

BLOOMSBURY SPORT
Bloomsbury Publishing Plc
50 Bedford Square, London, WC1B 3DP, UK
29 Earlsfort Terrace, Dublin 2, Ireland

BLOOMSBURY, BLOOMSBURY SPORT and the Diana logo are trademarks of
Bloomsbury Publishing Plc

First published in Great Britain 2023

A catalogue record for this book is available from the British Library

Library of Congress Cataloguing-in-Publication data has been applied for

ISBN: HB: 978-1-3994-0118-0; eBook: 978-1-3994-0120-3; ePdf: 978-1-3994-0119-7

2  4  6  8  10  9  7  5  3  1

Cover photographs courtesy of Louise Minchin, with the exception of:
Front cover – James Appleton (top), Vivienne Rickman (bottom left).
Back cover – Vivek Khanzode (right).
Author studio photograph by Rachel Joseph.

Typeset by Deanta Global Publishing Services, Chennai, India
Printed and bound in Great Britain by CPI Group (UK) Ltd., Croydon, CR0 4YY

To find out more about our authors and books visit www.bloomsbury.com
and sign up for our newsletters

*To the many courageous women whose stories are yet to be told, and to my own fearless friend Jay, without whose support and encouragement this book would never have been written.*

# Contents

# Fearless –
# The Back Story

It is 5.16 in the morning. I am balancing a bowl of congealed porridge in my left hand, juggling a pile of scripts in my right. I have to be dexterous, taking care not to drop the 40 pages because that will waste precious time. And time is not on my side.

The sheaf of paper is a printout of my briefing notes, packed with information which I need to speed-read for a dozen different interviews by 6 a.m. I am aware in the back of my mind that around six million people will be watching me presenting *BBC Breakfast*. As always, I need to get this right. The pressure is on.

The selection of guests and stories is pretty average for the show, something I am familiar with after nearly 20 years of waking up and going to work at 3.40 a.m. An interview with a government minister, an item on wind farms, 10 minutes with an '80s popstar making a comeback – and at the end, a classic, a programme perennial, an uplifting interview about a fearless endeavour.

Those stories are always my favourite part of the show.

This morning, it's about a brave man attempting to climb a mountain in his bare feet.

And that's when it hit me!

I surprise myself, saying out loud: 'Not again! What the actual hell?' (I've toned the swearing down; this is a book!)

Liz, who has expertly and with infinite patience been trying to do my make-up while my eyes flick across the words, asks: 'Are you OK?'

'No, I'm not, I've had enough! I cannot interview yet another man about his adventures! What about all the women doing incredible things? The fearless females? Why don't we talk to them? Why aren't they on the sofa being interviewed? Why don't we hear their stories?'

That was the moment for me, the moment I decided to write this book. I was fed up of being complicit with the narrative that it is only men who deserve to be celebrated, only men who are brave, only men who stretch the limits of what is humanly possible. I was done with telling only one side.

Why? Because being talked about and being seen matters. If you don't hear it and you don't see it, how can you be it? We need equal representation. I had to write this as a journalist, as an endurance athlete and as a mother to two daughters because, with respect to all the men I have interviewed, women and girls need heroes too. Heroes who look like them. And by the way, I'd argue that men like to hear the stories of heroic women too!

I had already fought and won some important battles for equality during my TV career, including a bruising and long-winded fight to get paid the same as my male co-presenters sitting next to me.

The other battle was to make sure that women presenting *BBC Breakfast* were allowed occasionally to lead the programme. I had noticed that almost every day my male colleague was given the prestigious task of saying hello at the top of each hour, introducing the programme, doing the first interview.

Once I had noticed how often it happened, I couldn't unsee it. Why was it happening? Why was I always the second person to speak, even though I was older and more experienced? What message did it send to all our female viewers? That I wasn't as important as my male counterpart? That I was second fiddle? That I didn't deserve to be there? What implication did that have for their own lives, and their own careers? I thought it was unfair, unequal and also immensely damaging.

So, I set out to try and change things, gently at first. I asked our (mostly male) directors if maybe, every now and then, I could start the programme? Ask the first question? Take charge of the most important story of the day? Some let me, others didn't. When they didn't, I asked why.

The most coherent answer they had was this: 'Because this is the way we have always done it.'

There it was: age-old, systemic discrimination built into the fabric of the programme.

For the next three months I took notes of dates and times, who did which interview and when. My hunch was right: it was almost always the man who took the lead. Armed with the facts I arranged a meeting with my boss at the time, which went like this.

'I have noticed that my co-presenter almost always seems to do the first interview of the day. Could we change it so I can do it occasionally?'

'That's not the case. They don't.'

I knew him well.

'I thought you might say that, so I've made notes. We can do one of two things. I can show these to you, and you can change it. Or you believe me and just change it?'

He never asked for my notes, and from that day on it was set in stone: every other day, the woman on the sofa was allowed to lead the programme, to be in charge.

I believe passionately that what you see in front of you matters: it shapes your view of the world and your value in it. That is why I was so incensed that the same thing that had happened to me was happening with one of my favourite parts of the programme. Almost every story about a bold or brave adventure starred a man.

That moment in Make-up, when my eyes were opened to the repeated pattern, galvanised me. I decided right then to go on a mission to find the women who were fearless, the women who were intrepid and courageous; those women whose stories had seldom been told; whose achievements had barely been recognised; and who had never had the opportunity to grace the famous red sofa and inspire us by sharing their experiences.

I would find them, talk to them, celebrate their stories.

As soon as I started, I was inundated with examples of courageous women from hugely diverse backgrounds. Undaunted women taking on awe-inspiring challenges: climbing the highest mountains, running superhuman distances, swimming in shark-infested waters just for fun and setting Guinness World Records while they did it. And doing this without praise, without accolade, without headlines or front pages, just because they were badass enough and fearless enough.

To get to the heart of who they are, and what motivates them, to be able to tell their stories better, I decided to do it the way that I know best, by taking part, spending time right beside them to experience the things they love.

Each chapter is dedicated to a different courageous woman and a different extraordinary adventure.

I have feared for my life while cycling across Argentina. I have gone freediving under ice in the pitch dark in Finland. I have found myself covered in mud playing rugby in the rain in southwest London. I have re-enacted the dangerous escape from Alcatraz and swum to San Francisco.

The women in this book have taken me far out of my comfort zone. It has been a roller coaster, both physically and emotionally. It has been exhilarating, inspiring and, sometimes, terrifying. I have learned so much, I have forged firm friendships and, best of all, I have been able to witness first-hand the indomitable power and tenacity of the female spirit.

This book is filled to the brim with inspiring stories of their endeavour, endurance, and bravery. *But* these fearless women are not alone. There are many others who deserve to be celebrated; many more than I can't fit into the pages of this book; many more that I would have liked to meet.

There are 18 women here. Follow their lead. Be inspired.

This is just the beginning.

*18 extraordinary women, 17 incredible adventures…*

# 1

# Anaya and Mitali Khanzode
## *Escape from Alcatraz*
### San Francisco

I feel like a really common misconception is we're fearless and we're not scared. I feel like we are scared.

I'm trying with all my might to pull myself through the choppy grey water, but the skyscrapers on the distant shore stay resolutely as far away as they were when I held my breath and jumped feet first off the side of a ferry. And now, even as I try to focus on them, the fog clinging to the city threatens to make them disappear. I am using every ounce of energy, breathing hard every second stroke, but it feels as if I am making no progress at all. I feel like I am stuck, going nowhere, unable to escape – as in one of my recurring nightmares where, despite all my increasingly desperate efforts, I can't get to where I want to go.

Something soft brushes gently against my left calf, almost caressing it. I think it must be another swimmer struggling as I am in the vast bay, but it feels different to the grasping hands

I am used to pulling at my feet in the washing-machine start of a triathlon. Different to the rough and tumble that is so familiar. I roll over onto my back to see if the person – I assume it is a person – who touched me is OK. There is no one behind me. Instead my view is filled by the foreboding sight of an inhospitable island. It is dominated by the shell of an imposing but dilapidated three-storey building. Perched in front is a lighthouse jutting out over the rocks, precariously but perfectly placed to warn passing shipping that this is a dangerous place, there are fast currents that can kill.

One glance at the distinctive rocky outcrop would tell you this is Alcatraz, America's infamous maximum-security prison where some of the most notorious gangsters, including Al Capone and Machine Gun Kelly, were incarcerated. Its fearsome reputation was immortalised by Clint Eastwood in the 1979 film *Escape from Alcatraz*.

The film is a dramatised account of an audacious attempt to escape from the penitentiary in June 1962 by Frank Morris and brothers John and Clarence Anglin. Over many months they hatched an elaborate plan to crawl through the air vents at the back of their cells, leaving dummy heads made of plaster and real human hair for the guards to find in their empty beds. After climbing through a ventilator shaft, onto the cellhouse roof, they shimmied down the bakery smokestack making their way to the shore. There, in the dead of night, they launched a makeshift raft, fashioned from stolen raincoats, into the water. They were never seen again. Whether they made it to safety is still a mystery. Investigators found debris of their raft and a packet of letters sealed in rubber, but their bodies were never recovered.

Right now, I am attempting to do what they tried to do: escape from Alcatraz and make my way to San Francisco but without the help of a raft.

Alcatraz is located on what is called The Rock, a site chosen to make its prisoners feel both psychologically and physically isolated. They were so close to land that when the wind was right they could hear laughter spilling into the night from the New Year's Eve parties in the Bay. A chill went down my spine hearing that on the island yesterday. It seems like an especially cruel kind of separation: to be so near but yet so far from freedom.

Right now, that's how I feel: isolated. I have no idea where my two companions are. We had braved the 1.8-metre leap off the deck of the Red and White ferry within seconds of each other, but fighting the current, in the choppy dark water I lost them as the horn sounded to mark the start of the race. They are nowhere to be seen in these relentless, nausea-inducing waves.

I knew it would be unlikely we would stay together. Anaya Khanzode is a world-class swimmer and had told me that she would make a break for it and try to get out ahead of the group, all 200 of us. Mitali, her older sister, is fast too but said she would be more likely to stay mid-pack. Right now, there seems to be no pack at all – or if there is one, I am not in it. I seem very alone in this expansive waterway, and after that brush on my calf, I am trying not to imagine what other creatures might be keeping me company in the water.

Of the infamous legends of Alcatraz, one of the most repeated, is that it is surrounded by shark-infested waters, a terrifying prospect. I know that sharks live here, and tried to calm my fears via Google. According to what I can find, it is shark *inhabited*, rather than *infested*. There have been no reports of attacks on swimmers for many years. Which seemed reassuring enough when I was safely at home researching on my computer, but not so reassuring now that I am all alone floating in the middle of an expanse of very deep and very dark water.

Both Anaya and Mitali admitted they have similar fears.

As we huddled together on the stone steps of the stands overlooking the circular bay of the Maritime National Historical Park, Anaya told me:

'It is really hard not to think *What is under me?*, because you can't see anything. I feel like a really common misconception is we're fearless and we're not scared. I feel like we are scared.'

Mitali backed her up. 'Yeah, we just hide it a lot better, we have irrational fears and there are things that can put us off. Like last time I swam there were lots of jellyfish. They don't sting or anything, they are moon jellyfish, but don't worry, they shouldn't even touch you. We never even see them.'

At the time of this conversation, I was sitting wrapped up in my dry robe ahead of the swim beside the two of them. The mention of jellyfish did nothing to calm my rising nerves, nor did Anaya's next comment.

'I'm much more scared of hypothermia because that's a very real thing that could happen. I think to myself, *OK, a shark is not going to bite me*. You know what I mean? But I could very easily get hypothermic. We take it really seriously, because we swim skins. So, if we are cold, we are, like, *we're getting out.* If I can't move my fingers, I know I am too cold.'

I am taking no chances with hypothermia today. I am not doing this swim in skins; I haven't trained enough in cold water. *Skins* means that all they will be wearing for the challenging crossing is a swimming costume and a hat. By contrast, I am zipped into a wetsuit that covers me from my wrists to my toes. It should be more than enough to keep me warm. The water today is expected to be about 17°C, a similar temperature to the sea in Cornwall in the summer – and cold enough to take my breath away. Not something I want to experience today.

Mitali and Anaya didn't always swim in skins. When they first started on their open-water journey, they had to wear surf wetsuits, because they were so young that they couldn't find triathlon or swimming wetsuits small enough to fit them. Anaya was only 8 when she swam her first Alcatraz, and Mitali 10. When I meet them, they are 17 and 20 respectively – and Anaya has done the swim we are attempting today 77 times and Mitali 76. She missed one of the races last year because she had COVID.

Since they first started training with Water World Swim, they have gone from strength to strength and are now both accomplished long-distance swimmers. Three years ago, in tandem, they swam the challenging 16-kilometre Strait of Bonifacio between Corsica and Sardinia. It took them four hours, 25 minutes to navigate strong currents and vicious stinging jellyfish. Anaya has recently swum 17.7 kilometres across Lake Tahoe which, because it is at altitude, makes the distance even tougher.

I ask Mitali what persuaded them to start their swimming careers here in San Francisco, tackling one of the most infamously dangerous bays in the world, over and over again.

'I think it is the reputation that comes with Alcatraz, the prison, the escape attempts, the prisoners disappearing. It's the backstory. The reason they built a prison on Alcatraz was so no one could escape, and if they did, they would die. It is kind of awesome to be able to say I have done that not once, not twice but multiple times. I think once you have swum Alcatraz you have earned a lot of bragging rights. There is something iconic about its shock value.'

The girls are accompanied today by their mother, Leena. She is a bundle of enthusiasm and infectious positive energy, and I realised she was their mum when I saw her giving generous greeting hugs to friends. This is obviously a close-knit community. It feels warm and welcoming, as if I am in the middle of a huge extended family. Leena and her husband Vivek moved to America from Nagpur in Central India in the 1990s when they were in their early twenties, and they have lived here ever since.

Her daughters having a passion for swimming was something Leena never imagined. 'I am terrified of water. I used to take Mitali swimming when she was three or four years old, and she absolutely refused to get in the water. She had the same fear as I did, and we sat on the side of the pool for more than a month, basically trying to desensitise her. Eventually she got in and look, here we are now, and I can't keep them out of the water!'

Mitali told me, 'I don't remember being scared, but I do remember being very young, growing up with swimming. I started swimming competitively in the pool and then in open water, and once I started open water, I realised that the shoulder problems I had in the pool were really alleviated because it was very cold. It's almost like you're icing your body while swimming. I had a lot less trouble with my shoulders, so I was like, *OK, this is meant to be for me. This is where I deserve to be*, and after that I just started pursuing longer distance in open water rather than in the pool.'

Very quickly Anaya, who is three years younger, followed in Mitali's wake. 'As Mum didn't have time to take us to two different places, whatever Mitali liked I did the same, and I just really loved it. At the start Mum used to say, "It's dangerous, don't do this." I don't blame her. If I was a parent, I would do the same and say, "You are not getting in the water, this is very cold water and you're six years old." So, she was really apprehensive at first, but the coaches actually really helped. Yeah, they're super nice.'

At this point, and as if hearing our conversation, we were interrupted by a shout for silence from Coach Mike, in charge of the swim and about to deliver the safety briefing.

This race is called Swim with the Centurions. Today is the 20th annual opportunity for anyone to swim with those who are aiming to make the crossing 100 times. There is a round of applause for Levy who is 76 years old and about to do his 91st swim. It's clear that he is much-loved. Anaya tells me she has to jump from the ferry directly behind him, because someone has landed on him before, and he only trusts her not to do so.

The first thing that is clear from the briefing is that safety is paramount. It needs to be. The tides between Golden Gate Bridge and Bay Bridge are fast and furious, and when the current is at its peak, it can run at 6 knots per hour. Put simply, if you didn't swim a stroke, you would be swept a mile downstream in less than 10 minutes. It goes without saying that someone unlucky enough to be caught in the water with no rescue boats on hand, wouldn't stand a chance. That and the threat of sharks are two of the reasons Alcatraz was such an effective place for preventing prison escapes. The environment is lethal.

The timing of our swim is going to be crucial. We will be getting into the water on a dying ebb tide, which means if we are fast enough, we can take advantage of the slack to get to the beach within about 40 minutes. If not, we will be carried away from our target (and towards Treasure Island) by the incoming tide – or, as Coach Mike more alarmingly calls it, 'the flood'. He takes out a huge map with arrows showing the different stages of the tide. If you can time it right, there is pretty much a straight line from Alcatraz to the Fontana Towers, which stand like homing beacons behind us.

If any of us are what the coaches describe as 'aquatically challenged' – a slower swimmer – the likelihood is that we will be pushed in the wrong direction by the flood, and will have to take a longer, curving route. If we stray too far and get dangerously out of position, the kayakers will pick us up and reposition us for our own safety.

'They are not trying to ruin your day!' Mike insists.

The currents aren't the only issue: the channel we are navigating is also a busy shipping lane. The day before our swim I had watched eyes wide in horror as a vast ship laden with containers cut through the water at some speed, exactly where we will be swimming today. Coach Mike reassures us that the Coastguard knows our intentions, so there should be no big ships coming through this morning. We also have what he calls a flotilla of fishing boats, kayaks, paddleboarders and two cops from the San Francisco Police Department on jet skis to escort us. I love it!

While there is no mention of sharks, there is talk of sea lions. Coach Pedro, the older statesman of Water World Swim, says there is no need to be concerned. 'We very seldom see them, especially if there is a group of people swimming. They don't approach anybody. If you're swimming by yourself, they get closer to you. But we have done various events and we haven't seen anybody be approached by a sea lion.'

I have seen the size of the sea lions that live here: they are ginormous and not to be messed with! I have watched them sunning themselves lugubriously in piles, their cumbersome bodies stacked on top of each other on the wooden slats of the piers. Some of them look the size of fully grown hippos. I don't need to encounter one in the water.

The atmosphere on our 20-minute journey to Alcatraz is an intoxicating mix of nervous excitement and camaraderie. We made a strange sight doing what Coach Mike described as the 'massive march' to the ferry, either bare foot or in flip-flops and carrying only goggles and swimming caps, looking out of place among the early morning jet-lagged tourists visiting Fisherman's Wharf.

Now we are passengers on board, we look even more strange. Apart from a handful of volunteers and supporters, including my husband David, everyone is either dressed in a swimming costume, Speedos or a wetsuit. As we stand chatting and jostling for space, I can feel the temperature rising from the body heat of bare arms, shoulders and torsos. It is a strange sensation; I have never been surrounded by so many people wearing so little. It feels like a warm and wonderfully unselfconscious celebration of the human body in all its shapes and sizes. Most of us are sporting bright green swimming hats and I notice Anaya has a white one. She tells me that everyone under 18 must take one. It is an extra safety precaution for the youngest among us, and I suppose it makes them easier to spot in the water.

I ask them both how they are going to navigate the infamous currents.

Anaya says: 'I feel like we have the upper hand, we have done it so many times, it just feels like we know what to do. Wherever you feel like being pushed, you have to adjust accordingly. You just want to feel the water. The water doesn't lie, so if you feel the water, you will know where to go.'

Mitali explains it a similar way. 'I have been swimming for longer than 12 years, and since we have been swimming for so long, we know what almost all of the different types of currents feel like and what to do.'

The way they speak – echoing each other's thoughts, one picking up where the other left off without so much as a pause for breath – is enchanting. They remind me of the way best friends can have a telepathy and finish each other's sentences. Anaya is the one that carries on when I ask what they mean by 'feeling' the water.

'I think it is one of our little like secret talents, that we can both be in the water for a minute or two and we could tell you how many knots the current is and the temperature down to the degree. Yeah, it's pretty cool, we are very good at that, I think we have had to get good at it.'

There is no time for more of their welcome advice. Our chat is interrupted when, much earlier than I had anticipated, the throbbing of the engine below our feet comes to an abrupt stop. I can feel my heart rate rising with nerves, which are not helped by a few anxious minutes of waiting and listening for instructions. We were warned that this would happen, that the captain would be coordinating with the Coastguard to decide where to drop us.

I see a double door on the side of the ferry open on my left and then bodies press against me, pushing me forwards towards the exit. There is no easy way to turn back now. It is all too late. I am going to have to jump, or I will be pushed over the edge. We have been told make the leap two by two, leaping away from each other so as not to cause any injuries. I am right behind Anaya and Mitali as they jump in together, perfectly in sync. I wait a couple of seconds and then feel the hand of a volunteer on my shoulder. Time to go.

I don't look down but look ahead towards Bay Bridge, raising one hand as if in alarm with the other pressed against my goggles to make sure they don't get pulled off my face. When I surface, spluttering and trying to make sense of where I am, I can feel the current pulling me like a magnet towards the ferry. I don't want to be pushed up against its sharp bow which rears alarmingly above my head. I can feel it drawing me in and struggle to get out of the way. I can see I am not alone; Mitali and Anaya are trying to do the same.

I have just managed to manoeuvre myself out of the way when I hear the loud blast of the second klaxon rippling across the water, heralding the start of the race. There are no words from anyone; in unison we put our heads down and swim.

I always find it hard to control my breath and settle into a manageable pace at the start of any race, but there is nothing more alarming than being dropped in a swathe of deep dark water with nothing between you and the shore over 2 kilometres away. I feel discombobulated, not sure of where I am going and breathless. The rising feeling of alarm makes my lungs constrict, and the fact that it is much choppier than I had expected doesn't help. I am being buffeted by nausea-inducing waves.

I try to settle myself down and swim steadily. It's not working, and that alarming brush of something along my calf, followed by an accidental gulp of salty water when I rolled over to see if it was another swimmer, has made things worse. The double rush of adrenaline and rising panic switch my brain into survival mode. I need to concentrate and use my skills and experience to get myself out of here. I remember what I have been told by both the girls and the safety crew: head for the Towers. I can just about see the dark shape of the square buildings in the far distance and set my course, but they seem an impossibly long way away.

As I calm myself down, I think over what they have both said about swimming being their happy place and remind myself it is mine too, if only I could relax and start enjoying it.

Anaya told me that the cold water particularly is a very important part of her life, a vital stress-reliever. 'This is the only place where I feel like I am, truly, truly happy. Nothing from school or my personal life is bothering me, and I am in the water, just swimming and being in the present moment. This is the only place where I can really, truly do that. It is also the thrill, the fun of it. We are thrill seekers.'

Mitali feels the same. 'This is very therapeutic and relaxing for us, because it forces you to think on your feet and to be fully present in the moment. Swimming is not like academic work; it is more spontaneous. You get to use more of your critical thinking in an on the fly manner. It feels like you use different parts of your brain or different ways of thinking to succeed. And that is really good for us.'

That thought about being present, makes me stop for a moment and take in the view. I tread water and with my head slightly above the waves am delighted to see that I am at last making good progress; I am about halfway across. Alcatraz is falling into the distance behind me, and a squadron of pelicans are wheeling above me. The way they fly, necks tucked in and wings outstretched, reminds me that their ancestors are dinosaurs.

To my right I can see the unmistakable ochre towers of the Golden Gate Bridge suspended in the fog. It is eerie but beautiful. Ahead of me is the metropolis of San Francisco. Now I am a bit closer, I can make out some of its extraordinarily steep streets which look almost vertical from my position semi-submerged in the Bay. It looks like an optical illusion – but having struggled to walk up them, I know it is not. I chuckle to myself at the sight of two San Francisco Police Department officers scudding about on their jet skis, blue lights flashing. The whole scene is surreal but brilliant.

I would have loved to have been able to swim alongside Anaya or Mitali, but in my confusion I have lost both of them, so I carry on alone. The current seems to have weakened as have the waves. I am finding it easier and feel more relaxed until my left hand bounces off a jellyfish I hadn't seen in the murk. It gives me another frisson of fright but, as they promised, it doesn't sting, and I continue making solitary progress.

When, finally, the seawall marking the entrance to Municipal Pier is within striking distance, I catch the welcome sight of another swimmer in front of me. I can see they are making steady headway. They have a powerful, rhythmic stroke and their strong kick is making an impressive wake of white water behind them. I try to accelerate to see if I can catch them up, and slide into their slipstream. When I get closer, I notice a bit more detail. They are wearing a white hat, and I spot the straps of a pink swimming costume crossed over their back. Wow!

I know Anaya was wearing a white hat and remember the flash of her pink swimming costume as she jumped off the ferry. What are the chances that I would find her 300 metres from the finish? Is it her? I can't be sure, but I am not losing a companion now. I stick like a shadow behind the swimmer, delighted that they are taking a perfectly straight line towards the flags marking the exit on the beach. They clearly know what they are doing, and I feel safe with them. The water is flatter and feels warmer. This is the type of swimming I love; I have found my happy place.

I stumble onto my feet, dripping and dizzy, half a second behind the anonymous swimmer and run as best I can across the sand to the official finish line. I see Leena on my left running too, chasing Anaya, rushing to get a photo. My gut instinct was right; it *was* her just ahead of me. Unbelievable!

We hug each other in celebration as glittering silver medals with a giant sea lion emblazoned on the front are hung around our necks. I see Anaya whisper something to her mum, who scoots off immediately to fetch her an inhaler. I had noticed her coughing earlier but didn't know she has asthma. That makes me even more in awe of her achievements.

Mitali is a couple of minutes behind us and the first thing she says is: 'Did you see the sea lions? One kind of brushed my leg, so I stopped with a kayaker, who said I was surrounded by them. They are not aggressive, they are so nice. Usually they are small, and they like to play with you. They always feel really gentle, it feels like an arm or something.'

That explains the mysterious caress I had felt along my leg! She has described it perfectly: so gentle it couldn't have been a human hand. Not only have I swum from Alcatraz, but on the way I have also had a close encounter with a sea lion!

We wait for the medal ceremony, wrapped up in towels and robes and with our teeth chattering from the cold. There is a special prize given to a girl who is only 10 and who has just swum her first Alcatraz. She was inspired to do it specifically by seeing Anaya and Mitali, and is made up when they stand with her for a photo, beaming on either side.

They are touched too.

I ask Mitali what it feels like to be a role model. 'We don't see many people like us, especially in this sport. We are young women, we are people of colour, that is just not common in the sport at all. And so, it's nice being representative of that in some way, and we are very aware of it. But at the same time this is just something we do for fun. It is great that it has an impact on young swimmers, but we do it first and foremost because we love it and everything else comes second.'

I bid goodbye to them as they chat to the 10-year-old who is smiling as much as they are, and I walk away with the knowledge that their legacy is safe. They are making waves in the world of swimming, which will continue to ripple.

In the Bay behind them, the tide is now in full flood, whipping past Alcatraz towards Bay Bridge. Small sailing boats are scudding over the water, sails billowing and making use of the strong tide and the blustery wind. If we were swimming now, we would have no chance of safely making the crossing, we would all be swept away, helpless, downstream. I think about those audacious prisoners who entered the Bay in the dead of night, whose bodies were never found. Could they have made it? From what I know of these foreboding waters, I think it highly unlikely.

I walk back to Fisherman's Wharf buoyed by endorphins, and celebrate by tucking into a steaming fish chowder served inside a warm, hollowed-out sourdough loaf. I remember what Mitali says about bragging rights as I look at my medal and think they are the ones that deserve them, not me.

# 2

# Christine Grosart
## *Wild Caving*
### The Mendip Hills

> The cave doesn't judge you, the cave is a real leveller. It doesn't care what you do for a living, it doesn't care how much money you have. . . Basically, the challenge is between you and the cave.

I have never been more delighted to see the light of day. Emerging from the darkness, I feel as if I have been reborn, that I have escaped from a nightmare. If it weren't for the carpet of stinging nettles around me, I would throw myself on the ground and hug it. My body is buzzing with adrenaline, but not the kind I like. It is induced by fear, which I have been trying to keep under control for four long hours.

'There is not enough money in the world to persuade me to do that *ever* again!!' I say to Christine and Jackie, who have been with me for the whole time.

Christine laughs, and I can see from Jackie's reaction she feels exactly the same. To say I have been out of my comfort zone is an understatement.

I have spent the day wild caving with one of the most extraordinarily brave and intrepid people I have ever met: Christine Grosart. Before we left, she explained wild caving to me.

'Wild caving is the real deal; it is not a tourist type of caving; you can't just switch the light on and have a quick exit if you don't like it. The way in, is the way out. There is no short cut and there are no emergency exits.'

Christine is an off-shore paramedic who dedicates her spare time to cave-diving, exploring small spaces and tunnels underground. She has squeezed, crawled and pulled herself into places in the world that few other humans dare to reach, and she is passionate about introducing others to the joys of her favourite pastime.

'Cave-diving is a little too far out of the public's reach for them to understand. They will look at it and go *Yes you are mad* and then they don't want to know any more about it. Trying to explain what we do takes too long, and they can't comprehend it. That is why I love taking people caving because you just get a taster of what it is really like.'

A taster is what I have had, and despite her valiant efforts to persuade me to love it, I don't think I ever will.

Christine, in stark contrast, pretty much always has.

'I started caving when I was about 14 or 15. I suppose it was a family affair. My uncle was in a caving club when he was a youth. And my mother always spent time around the caving club as well. When I had time off and I did come home, I would go to the caving club in the Mendips, because that was the only way I could get to see my mother and my uncle. It was fun, you would go to the pub, go caving, have a bit of a weekend of it. It was a really social affair.'

When I imagined going caving, I had pictured myself walking into a vast spacious cavern, navigating my way over rocks and boulders towards the back of it, and only then might I possibly have to start crawling and squeezing myself between crevices. Not for a second did I imagine that I would start the day by having to lower myself into a small triangle hewn into limestone, that I would be immediately plunged into a darkness only faintly lit up by my headtorch, feeling for a safe foothold on a slippery platform while wearing wellington boots. That first tricky manoeuvre is quickly followed by a precipitous climb down a 2.5-metre wall with what feels like very little space between me and the ceiling.

I am only a few metres into the cave, and I already feel like the weight of the world is pressing in on me, about to crush me. My anxiety levels have gone from 6 to 10 in less than a minute.

I don't like small spaces at all. I hate them. Especially small spaces with other people in them. Today was going to be very challenging.

Jackie, who won a caving experience in a charity auction, is also feeling anxious about today's excursion because she suffers from vertigo.

I ask Christine if the fears are normal?

'In caves everybody has a thing they don't like, and it can depend on your physique. Some people don't particularly like abseiling on a rope because they don't like heights. Some people are frightened of squeezes. They are frightened of small, tight bits.

'For me, personally, the thing I hate the most is boulder hopping. There is a cave in South Wales called Ogof Draenen, which is one of the most beautiful in the whole country. But to get there is about five hours of muddy, greasy, off-balance, ankle-breaking boulders, and it just goes on forever. It is physically draining, and it is mentally draining because you know that one false move and you will break an ankle. I hate it.

'I hate it because it is dry, hot, sweaty, slippery. Some tall people don't like crawling, as their femur is so long; they prefer to crawl flat out on their belly. Short people don't like doing traverses. That is when you are between two walls, and you have your fingertips on one side and your toes on the other and you sort of bridge across it. Tall people will just run across it and some shorter people imagine they will plummet into the abyss.'

We are in the longest cave system in the Mendip Hills, Swildon's Hole. It stretches 9,000 metres beneath the picture-book village of Priddy in Somerset. A stream runs all the way through the cave and resurfaces at the much better-known cave system at Wookey Hole, a couple of miles from where I am now. (The course was dye-traced by pouring colour into the water, which emerged 24 hours later at Wookey.)

This cave, which started life as a coral reef under the sea millions of years ago, was first explored in 1901. In the intervening years many hundreds of cavers have squeezed their way in because it is, as Christine explains, a classic cave.

'Most cavers in the UK will have been here because it has everything. You can do an easy dry route without getting your feet wet (ish), or you can take a blood-curdling trip in there which will take you hours. It has cave diving at the end. It has something for everyone.'

I am hoping today that there won't be any blood curdling, but I am not convinced.

The entrance to the cave is surprisingly nondescript. The opening I have just squeezed through is covered by a grey stone blockhouse hidden out of sight in a dip in a beautiful, wooded valley. There is no big sign saying *Danger, Risk to Life* or *Enter at Your Own Risk*. None of the 21st-century health and safety warnings I had expected to see. Instead, there is an innocuous metal plaque on the outside wall which says simply:

Mendip Cave Rescue
In the event of an accident or emergency dial 999, ask the police for CAVE RESCUE, give details and wait for call back from Mendip Cave Rescue

I am heartened to read the last line: '1936–2011, 75 years of cavers rescuing cavers'.

I hope their expertise is not going to be necessary today but am relieved to see they have years of experience getting people out.

Christine has already taken me through the safety procedures and what to do in an emergency. The biggest worry is that our lights go out. If they do, we'll be in big trouble.

'It sounds obvious, but without light it is really dark, pitch black, as black as it could ever be. If your light fails or goes out, you are stuffed.

'If your lights do fail while you are diving, you have a piece of string to follow under the water. On a cave dive you can't sit there and wait because you will run out of air, and you will drown. But in a dry cave, following a piece of string in the dark is not going to help you, as you will trip over or fall down a hole.

'If your light goes out and you are in complete blackness, you have no option but to stay put, sit down and do nothing. Because if you walk five yards that way, you could fall down a vertical drop or a pitch. You don't know where you are; you could be going *into* a cave or *out* of a cave. You never, ever try to get yourself out in the dark, it will end badly. So, we always take a spare light in this pot that one of you will be carrying. Light failure underground is serious, it is critical.'

I ask if we can turn our lights out to see how dark it is when we are in the cave. I am not sure why I ask that, given my nerves around the whole expedition. Later, as the three of us are perched uncomfortably on rocks underground in one of the larger caverns, we all switch our specialist headtorches off simultaneously.

It is a shock.

We are engulfed by a thick, choking wave of coal-black darkness. My eyes search in vain to make out the shapes of the rocks that I know are there, but in front of me there is nothing but a void, not even the slightest glimmer of light. The claustrophobia crushes me. Nausea sweeps over me, exacerbated by the thundering of water gushing malevolently in the distance. The air I desperately pull into my lungs feels uncomfortably warm, too hot to breathe, depleted of oxygen. I feel blind, lost, helpless – and very far from rescue.

Before it becomes too much, Christine saves me. After less than a minute, she tells us to switch our lights back on, and my whole body shudders with relief. I now understand why I shouldn't move if my torch fails. The cave is a deathtrap: without being able to see, any step I take could be lethal.

It is not just head torches that Christine has lent us for the trip. I am kitted from head to toe in caving paraphernalia. The only thing I am wearing that is my own is my swimming costume. Over it, I have a royal-blue fluffy onesie made from fleece which makes me look as if I am wearing a giant Babygro.

'Just wear a swimming costume, you must have no cotton, no T-shirts. If they get wet, you will get very, very cold. The fleece drains water very quickly from your top half, it drains into your wellies, and you will have wet feet all day, but that is just caving. But you won't be saturated, the fleece will be warm and comfy.'

I love the matter-of-fact way Christine talks me through things. As well as the fleece, she gives me what she called 'wet' socks to put on.

'These are neoprene socks, so when your feet get wet, they will keep them lovely and toasty, really warm but not dry. Once you have them on, you put on your tough oversuit over the top, then finally you put your wellies on. We use wellington boots because they are rubber, they are grippy, it doesn't matter if they get wet, they are extremely rugged, they provide ankle support. Wellies are the go-to for cavers, even in exploration, we use wellies. If water gets in, you can just bend your leg and tip it out.'

My outfit is completed with kneepads, a belt that looks a bit like a diver's belt and a safety helmet.

We laugh at ourselves as we walk over meadows towards the entrance in blazing sunshine. With me wearing my red overall and her in her matching blue one, we look like a curious blend of mechanics and Teletubbies.

Right from the moment I squeeze myself through the narrow hatch, I feel out of place. Like I have fallen through a trapdoor and landed on another planet, slipped into an alien environment where I am small and insignificant and stupid. In the rocks I see faces which are watching my every move, mocking my ignorance. As we squirm through narrow tunnels, and small spaces, Christine talks me through very clearly and very carefully, telling me exactly how to get around all the obstacles in our way.

'Put your foot here, grasp that ridge with one hand, bend your knees, twist your head and push.'

She explains carefully how to manoeuvre through the appropriately named Lavatory Pan.

'You are going to have to do a Superman move to get through it. As you crawl into it, you have to have one arm in front of you and one arm behind you. Then, using your toes, you have to sort of levitate yourself up against the water. There really isn't any form of foothold, so you have to shimmy your way against gravity using the pressure of your body against the rock.'

I feel as if I am trying to solve a dangerous 3-D jigsaw puzzle and I am one of the pieces. Only if I make the right shape, at the right time, will I get through safely. I have never been more grateful for my bottom, which helps me push upwards through the water that is being flushed over me, hence the name. Christine has mentioned how much difference your physique can make and, thankfully, this cave suits me: I am tall, and my long arms and legs are making the climbing and reaching easier for me than it is for Jackie, who is shorter.

The experience is so foreign to me, so unnatural and so terrifying, I ask Christine if she thinks you need a particular type of personality to love being underground.

'Hmm,' she says, 'yes, you need to be a weirdo!'

She guffaws with laughter, and then goes on to explain what she means.

'Caving is a niche activity. Most people do it once at school or with the Scouts. And then they never go again. And they think it is just one of those things you do once, they don't realise you can actually take it up and join a club and spend your weekends underground. But cavers who love it have found a sport that doesn't discriminate. You either fit or you don't when you get down a cave. It is not competitive, the cave doesn't judge you, the cave is a real leveller. It doesn't care what you do for a living, it doesn't care how much money you have. It doesn't care who you are. Basically, the challenge is between you and the cave. Because of that it is a close-knit, non-judgemental community.'

For Christine, caving is her life. She tells me she has no children, no partner, and no ties because she has chosen to spend almost every minute of her free time dedicated to cave exploration.

'I don't think I could do what I do if I had those things. It takes me a whole year to set up one expedition and as soon as it is finished I start setting up again. My whole life, all my money goes into that expedition. If I go at it half-hearted, I wouldn't get the funding, I wouldn't get the support, so I have made a personal choice over what is most important to me.

'I have 10 lifetimes worth of things that I want to do on this planet, and I am trying to cram them all in now, I have one life and I am living it. Maybe a bit of that comes from being a paramedic because I see people die younger than me . . . it really is a case of making every day count.'

When I meet her for our underground adventure, she is about to head off on an ambitious expedition to Croatia, where she is in the process of exploring a cave system with a series of underwater sumps and connecting tunnels. So far, they have got to the end of Sump 2, a submerged passageway 50 metres deep and 600 metres long, which is filled with cold water at a life-threatening temperature of 7°C. The only way to get through it is by using deep-diving scuba equipment and battery-powered handheld scooters to propel the divers, and all their equipment, through the water deep under the rocks. It sounds to me like a lethal combination of horror movie and James Bond.

The ultimate goal for Christine, her mission in life, is to find undiscovered, virgin caves.

'Exploring somewhere that no one has ever stood, is the pinnacle for me. When we look at exploration, I think we look at things like the ocean trenches and tops of mountains, but you can map those. You know where they are, you know what they look like, so all you need to do is aim at them. The thing with exploration underground is you don't know what is there, you can't see it on a satellite, you can't see it on a robotic camera underwater. You have to be there; you have to physically go and find it. These underground spaces are the last frontiers on earth, and I want to be the one to discover them.'

She is nervous ahead of her big expedition, but when I speak to her on her return I can see it written all over her face: she is exhausted but ecstatic. I am delighted for her because she has achieved even more than she wanted: she has discovered one of the most significant cave systems found in Croatia in the last 20 years. Over a series of what she calls 15-hour push-days, the divers managed to get through to Sump 8, which is over 2.5 kilometres deep into the rock and which opens into a vast cavern with boulders the size of buses. No one had ever been there before. She is thrilled but also overwhelmed; now she feels the pressure to plan a bigger expedition to get past that cavern and find the end of the cave. It is a monumental task.

And I'm not going to be able to help. Here, in the Mendip Hills, I'm relatively safe – and unimaginably scared, grateful for the moments of respite.

With no warning, we arrive at the entrance of a large cavern, and I look up to see what seems like acres of space above my head. I breathe a deep sigh of relief, then gasp in astonishment at the depth of the colours, the reds, the ambers and ochres running down seams from the ceiling. I am entranced by the delicate stalactites hanging from the rugged, misshapen roof and the stalagmites rising to meet them. Mesmerised by the way the waxy calcium carbonate deposits seem to have settled like a cream-coloured blanket over the sharp edges of the rocks, smoothing them over. What I am most taken with are the tiny, gossamer light straws – ethereal stalactites the circumference of a droplet of water.

As we turn back to start our journey to the surface, my claustrophobia takes control. I know we are over two hours into the cave, and it is going to take us two hours to get out. I am trying hard to marshal my thoughts, and not let then run amok. I work out the best place for me to be is at the front. That way I know there is always going to be space ahead. Every time I squeeze successfully past another tight space, I sit down and get my breathing back under control and have a quiet word with myself.

*It's fine. Keep calm. Keep moving. You will get out. It will be easier if you don't panic.*

I am drawing on all my experiences of extreme situations. Trying to remember all I have learned, to keep myself in the moment, to keep focussed and stop my thoughts spiralling out of control. It takes a monumental effort to do so: my rational and emotional sides of my brain are in a furious back and forth tug of war. Right now, as I sit breathing slowly in the darkness, listening to Christine talk Jackie through another climb, the rational part is winning, but only just.

The first indication that I am going to get out safely is the unmistakable noise of a mosquito buzzing past. We must be close to the exit. Then I see black slimy slugs sliding over the wet stones – a surprisingly welcome sight, small signs of life meaning that we are close to daylight once again. I can feel the tension wash through my body into those wet welly boots.

In my last conversation with Christine, I have to apologise.

She has done her utmost to persuade me to love her sport, and I do – on paper. I love the idea of the extreme challenges it puts your body and brain through. I love that its community is close-knit, non-competitive, non-judgemental, and will put their lives on the line to save others. Just remember the boys trapped deep inside the flooded Tham Luang cave system; their rescue was spearheaded by some of Christine's friends. These are dedicated and selfless people.

So, I have to apologise because as much as she has tried, she can't convert me. I know she needs people to join her in her next assault on the Croatian caves, but I just can't be one of them.

I say goodbye and wish her luck and assure her I will be watching and cheering her on – from the safety of the sidelines.

# 3

# **Cath Pendleton**
## *Freediving Under Ice in the Dark*
### Finland

I have got to be honest with you, Louise, I was so stressed not being able to find a wetsuit in extra large that I was thinking of any excuse to get out of the trip. If you weren't going along with me, I would have got out of it!

I look down into a triangle of pitch-black water in the centre of a frozen lake in Finland. It has been hacked out of ice 1 metre thick with a jagged saw. The surface looks oily and glutinous. It is as ominous and as featureless as a black hole in outer space. I am overwhelmed by a sense of fear and foreboding. I reach out my hand to say: 'Cath, stop, don't do it!'

I'm a millisecond too late!

My freediving buddy has taken her final deep breath and disappeared under the surface. Her torch is gone, I can't see her, I can't reach her, and there is nothing I can do but hope that she is going to make it to the other side.

I can't rush the 15 metres to where she should emerge, it's too slippery. I'm scared I will fall, and I walk shakily. I am terrified. She is alone, somewhere in the depths of the lake beneath my feet. Time stretches and slows. I am confused. This is taking her ages, and I can't walk quickly enough.

My eyes are straining for any small sign of her; my brain is buzzing with scenarios that are all catastrophic. *Will she be trapped? How can I help her? Will I ever see her again?* Seconds feel like minutes.

I glimpse a flicker of a green light like a tiny butterfly, fluttering weakly through the packed ice, like a homing beacon. It can only be Cath; she must be moving; she's heading in the right direction; she must be on her way to safety.

I hear gasping before I see her.

'Fucking hell, I am never doing that again!' Quickly followed by: 'Sorry about the swearing!'

Cath Pendleton is a record-breaking ice swimmer – and that was her immediate reaction to her first ever freedive under ice.

'Breathe,' is what I say when I make it to her side. 'Breathe,' as I have been taught to do in my freediving training, and then: 'Thank God, you made it!'

Despite the relief, my heart constricts: now Cath is safe, it's my turn to take the plunge.

I love a challenge, and in addition I love pretty much anything that involves being submerged in water – but what I am about to do is a galaxy beyond anything I am used to.

Freediving under ice, in the dark, is the stuff of nightmares. Terrifying thoughts are running free in my head. *What if I run out of breath? Get lost? Get stuck? Can't get out?*

There is no turning back, though. I am dressed from head to toe in the thickest wetsuit I could find and about to take a deep breath, then pull myself under the ice in the hope that I make it to the other side.

Rewind a few months to when Cath first mentioned freediving in Finland. Back then, apart from worrying about the temperature of the water, I thought, *Well, how hard can it be?* I am a good swimmer, confident in open water, and a qualified scuba diver. The idea of combining all three together appealed to my sense of adventure. I assumed there was a level of risk involved and, of course, a bit of training – but I had no inkling about how dangerous it is, or what it takes to do it. No idea of the skills needed, or the courage.

It was when she sent me a link to where we were going that the penny began to drop. The location itself looks like a perfect setting for a scene from *Game of Thrones*. Lake Päijänne is the second largest lake in Finland. It is also the deepest. In some parts the water, which is so pure you can drink it, is over 90 metres deep. The lake is two hours' drive north from Helsinki, and in winter the forests and fields are blanketed in deep snow. A frozen wonderland.

The picture greeting me on the website, though, struck fear into me. It shows a diver emerging from water as dark as bitumen, encased in shiny steel grey neoprene. He is wearing a black mask with bubbles escaping and his piercing, glassy eyes look wild. The hint of a smile serves to scare me, not reassure me. I realise he has no oxygen tanks, and was holding his breath while swimming underneath the ice.

It dawns on me there is no way I can wing it; this is a serious undertaking. I read on and see that to take part in the event I must have a certification in freediving. *How on earth am I going to get that? And where?*

The short answer is: in a boiling hot swimming pool in Harrogate on a miserable Sunday night in February.

Freediving is a very dangerous sport and to do it safely you have to be taught by a qualified instructor, and always dive with someone else. This chapter is the ultimate in *DO NOT TRY THIS AT HOME!*

Thankfully, I manage to find an instructor, a guru in the world of freediving in the UK: Steve Millard from Apneists UK, based in Manchester. I think he thinks I'm utterly nuts when I tell him I have no freediving experience whatsoever and want to do my first dive in the dark under ice. Still, he isn't perturbed, and even though the timescale to get me qualified is tight, he takes me under his wing.

Before even getting into the pool at Harrogate Ladies College, I must get a doctor's certificate to say I am fit to dive, read a freediving manual and complete an online exam. I also have to do a whole series of breathing exercises and teach myself to hold my breath for long periods.

The first challenge is to find the time for the exercises. Finally, on a Sunday afternoon, I find a spare hour or so, and do as I was told: relax, get my breathing into a steady rhythm and then, when I feel ready, press go on the timer and hold my breath with my lungs full. The pressure builds very quickly in my chest as I watch the clock tick past 30 seconds, 40, 45. At 50, when I feel like I am going to explode, I breathe out and gasp for air.

According to Steve's instructions, that's just the start. The first 'hold' is just my gauge, I have to try and improve it, adding 15 seconds to every subsequent hold.

'Do three more breath holds with three minutes in between each one. After your fourth hold, have a five-minute break and then go for it, see what you can do. You might even surprise yourself!'

I do. By the end of that first session I manage to hold my breath for one minute, 30 seconds.

Before Steve will allow me into a pool, I have to let him know how my breath-holding is going. I tell him I am managing to get to one minute, 40 seconds, and am pretty pleased with myself until he asks me if I have had any contractions? I don't even know what he means! Turns out that until I have had contractions, I haven't tried hard enough.

I look it up. Contractions when you are holding your breath are involuntary spasms of the muscles in your diaphragm caused by the $CO_2$ building up to excessive levels. They are a sign your body is trying to force you to breathe out the $CO_2$ and replenish the oxygen. Some people feel as if they have tickling butterfly kisses in their chest; for others it's like a punch in the stomach.

The first time I have a contraction, it gives me a fright. I feel like the top of my ribcage and throat are being squeezed by invisible hands and I breathe out immediately in shock. The second time it happens, I realise I don't need to panic, I can hold my breath a little longer.

I ask Cath about what it feels like for her. She tells me she has never felt them at all, even when she has held her breath for two minutes, 40 seconds.

Trying to hold your breath lying on the floor when you are super- relaxed at home is one thing, though, and quite different to doing it underwater.

There are only three of us on our freediving course in Harrogate. Steve has a lovely dry sense of humour but makes it clear that he is going to ensure we all take this very seriously. The first rule of freediving is you must *always* dive with a buddy. Their job is to watch you very carefully, and if needs be, if something goes wrong, to rescue you.

I am paired up with Sarah and our first task is to do what is called a static dive, face down, not moving in the water. It is bizarre to be standing in the shallow end with my hand on her shoulder and watching my stopwatch tick through the seconds. I tap her to let her know when the minute has passed and then every 15 seconds. She is utterly still, so lifeless she looks like she has drowned. My brain goes into overload: *Is she OK? When will she come up? Should I pull her out?* Thankfully she comes up at the allotted time of one minute, 45.

It is my turn next. I get my breathing under control and then slowly sink into the water, hands suspended beneath me, eyes closed, trying to keep calm. After the initial rush of panic, I reach a quiet peace for a while, before the pressure in my chest builds, and I feel my lungs might burst.

When I come up, Sarah says, 'Breathe,' and I take three sharp intakes of air.

In the three hours we are in the sweltering pool I learn an extraordinary amount, including how to safely rescue from the bottom of the pool a diver who has blacked out. By the end of the session, I can swim three lengths underwater assisted by massive fins over 1 metre long. I feel like a mermaid, I love this sport.

By the time I finally meet up with Cath, I have moved from a static dive to being able to dive down to 5 metres in the deep diving pool in Leeds.

Like me, Cath is a newbie to freediving. Swimming in open water is her passion, particularly swimming in extremely cold water, and she is exceptionally good at it. In February 2020, she set a Guinness World Record for the Most Southerly Ice Swim (female), swimming one mile inside the Antarctic Polar Circle at a latitude of 66.6°S in Hanusse Bay, off Graham Land, Antarctica.

Before I met Cath, I didn't know what an ice mile was, but now I know that an official ice mile must be swum in temperatures of 5°C and below, and that the swimmer must wear only a swimming costume, a pair of googles and one hat. Cath completed her mile in the Antarctic in water at 0.03°C in 32 minutes, 54 seconds.

To be immersed at that temperature even for a couple of minutes is life-threatening. To stay in it for over half an hour and keep moving is a feat of endurance far beyond the limits of most humans.

Watching the documentary about her record attempt, *The Merthyr Mermaid*, I am impressed by her calm and focussed approach. She looks tiny and vulnerable against the giant icebergs.

'The water was just so blue. I was drinking the water. It wasn't salty. The top layer was like really blue, there was a lighter blue. It was incredibly clear; it was just beautiful. At one time a little tiny fleck of green came close to me that looked like a bit of moss or fern. That freaked me out because I thought, *If I can see that, what happens if I see an animal or something?* I didn't feel cold at all, that was the craziest thing. Normally when I get in and it is 3°C or 4°C, it feels like my hands have been slapped in a vice, and my teeth get really cold. But I got in, just shivered a bit, waited and then started swimming.'

She went into the water knowing that there were leopard seals nearby who had been feasting on penguins and, more alarmingly, just before she got in the water a pod of orca swam past the safety boat.

'I went through stages of *I am loving it* and then, *Oh my, something is going to eat me.* And then I would be calm again and be swimming along thinking, *I am so privileged to be here. So many people would love to be here, and it's me.*'

Cath was always a swimmer. She loved it from a very young age, and some of her earliest memories are of playing in the River Usk in Sennybridge. After having two daughters, she was brought back to the open water by triathlon. Her first ever swimming race was the Welsh Open Water Estuary Swim in 2013, when she completed a respectable 2 kilometres. She quickly progressed from there onto 5 kilometres, then 10 kilometres and in 2016 she swam Lake Windermere, a daunting 17.7 kilometres. She went on to swim the English Channel solo in 16 hours, 45 minutes – an experience about which she is very nonchalant. Laughing, she tells me it was really boring because she didn't see a thing.

Her first non-wetsuit cold water swim was in September 2015, her second just a couple of days later – and she was hooked. She had found her sport. 'I absolutely knew I wanted to do it all the time and I got completely addicted.'

I love swimming, and I love swimming in open water, but I am not one of those people who likes the cold or who chooses to swim through the winter without a wetsuit. The very thought makes me shiver, so I ask her to explain what makes it so special for her.

'The winter is my favourite time, because when it's really cold, it switches my busy brain off. Even when I am speaking to you, now, I've got things jumping in my head. In the summer when I swim, my head is still busy, I am a nightmare, I can't switch off, I am constantly thinking about what I have to do later, what is for dinner, this and that. But when it is really cold, I love it because it just switches off my brain completely: all I can do is concentrate on how I am feeling and how my body is feeling. It is my reset button.'

Once Cath discovered her true love in sport, she started swimming competitively, and that is when she first started making history. In January 2016 she became the first Welsh woman to swim an ice mile in Keeper's Pond in Blaenavon. She then went on to represent Team GB in the World Ice Swimming Championships in Murmansk in Russia, winning bronze in her category.

She is an incredible athlete – even though, as she puts it, her size means that some people might not think she looks like one. Given that her body has completed record-breaking swims and taken her on adventures all over the world, I ask her how she feels about it?

'I hate my body because I am so fat. But then I see pictures of me doing a triathlon and I used to think I was really fat then and I was only about 10 stone. I just see a fat blob and people always say I should celebrate it, but I can't. I have always had a problem with my weight, no matter what size I am.'

I am saddened to hear her. What she has achieved may not have changed her attitude towards herself, but she knows its impact has been hugely positive for other people. She tells me about a woman who came up to her when she was swimming at Lake 32 in the Cotswolds and said:

'Cath, I need to thank you because I've lived here for many years, and for about eight years I have wanted to come and swim, but I didn't want to put a wetsuit on because of my size. And I've seen you and what you have done, and I thought: *Fuck it, I'm going to phone them and ask if am allowed to swim there without a wetsuit.*'

'Of course, she could!' says Cath and then goes on to tell me that throughout that summer she saw the same woman swimming happily for an hour and a half at a time.

'Before, she just didn't have that encouragement to go and do it, and because of what she saw me doing, now she swims.'

Cath is a trailblazer, she changes people's perceptions of themselves, and she is doing the same for me. She is the only reason that I have for even one second contemplated freediving, let alone freediving under ice.

Even though we have both trained ahead of our trip we are both extremely nervous. Cath is nervous about her breath-holding because she has run out of time to train. She practises on the plane before we arrive, reinforcing her knowledge that she can hold her breath for well over a minute – way more than we should need under the ice.

I am worried about the cold for two reasons. Firstly, I have Raynaud's, which means my hands and feet can go numb after a 10-minute swim in water at 20°C, so there is no way I will be able to feel them in ice-cold water. Secondly, I haven't acclimatised myself to cold water as I should have.

I have tried – and failed. I have managed to persuade myself to get in the cold water only twice, and each time I squealed more than I breathed. I know that cold water makes me panicky, it squeezes my lungs, and it takes my breath away – which is exactly what you don't need when you are freediving. Being able to hold your breath is the key to success, so the cold could be my nemesis.

One thing we do have on our side is *very* thick wetsuits. As a seasoned ice swimmer, Cath would rather dive without one, but safety is a priority and she has been asked to wear one for the event.

Getting into our wetsuits is itself an ordeal. To keep us warm and to enable us to swim, we are using suits designed for freediving which are open cell and have an integrated hood. An open cell wetsuit has no inner lining, meaning that the neoprene goes right up against the skin to create tiny suction cups that stick to the skin, and the advantage is they keep you warmer and drier – it's impossible for water to get in. The massive disadvantage is that because they are dry on the inside, they are incredibly hard to get on. The surface is sticky and rubbery and clings to anything it touches. Try sliding that over your skin and hair! You basically can't.

Before we had even left for Finland, we both posted picture after picture on our group WhatsApp showing us in various states of distress and disarray after trying to squeeze into our wetsuits. The only way to do it is to lubricate the inside with something like hair conditioner and then pull it on very, very gently. The first time I tried, I didn't use enough and got trapped inside unable to get my head through the hood, which got stuck on my hair. I couldn't get it on or off, and thought I was going to suffocate before I even got anywhere near the water! Thankfully my daughter Mia heard my shouts from the bathroom and ran to help me out.

For Cath, it was even more difficult. She couldn't find one in her size and ended up with five different suits, one of which was sent all the way from Spain. The experience was so stressful, she nearly reconsidered the whole trip.

'I have got to be honest with you, Louise, I was so stressed not being able to find a wetsuit in extra large that I was thinking of any excuse to get out of the trip. If you weren't going along with me, I would have got out of it!'

I have never been to Finland, and neither has Cath, so it is all new to us. Our trip is in early March, so the country is still locked in winter, and everything is covered in a thick blanket of white. As we drive north from Helsinki, the city gives way to vast featureless snowfields interspersed by isolated wooden houses and farms with metal roofs painted a rusty red. It is beautiful but desolate. I wouldn't survive for long here outside the car.

By the time we wend our way to the lake, it is already sunset, and we are only just in time for our first dive. As quick as we can, we gather all our stuff together for a briefing and realise we will have to hire more weights. The thickness of our wetsuits, added to the natural buoyancy of our bodies, means that we are going to need to carry some ballast on a belt to weigh us down. Without it, we won't be able to get deep enough in the water to pull ourselves under the ice.

For an extreme sport, with lots of potential dangers, the safety briefing is surprisingly laid-back. We are told the dive site is a walk of about 150 metres into the middle of the frozen lake and that we don't need to worry about finding it, even though it is now pitch dark, as it is lit by burning wooden torches. There will be a series of ice holes, set in pairs opposite each other, 15 metres apart and connected by a system of underwater ropes. We must clip ourselves onto the rope with our safety lanyards attached to our wrist. That means we can't get lost under the ice, and if anything should happen to us, we can be found and rescued quickly.

Our kit is checked to confirm we have what we need; we have to prove we have our underwater torch and our lanyard. I think I have everything.

Getting into our wetsuits is a nightmare. We go into the sauna and have help to sluice conditioner all over the inside, then we start the process of squeezing ourselves in. For Cath it is really hard, and it takes three of us working together to pull the bottoms up. We are laughing as we do it, but she is mortified and her feelings are not helped by another diver who isn't in our group of four telling her she should have a suit custom made for her

'I was really stressed when we got there because I was embarrassed. I couldn't get into the wetsuit on my own, and I was shattered that it took three of us to get me in there.'

It feels like we have been transported to the scene of a medieval sacrifice as we walk towards the bright, flickering flames dancing in the distance. We can hear the murmur of voices as the snow crunches beneath our footsteps. It is piled 30 centimetres deep on top of the ice and has a hard crust to it which cracks under my feet. The cold is already creeping up through the soles of my Crocs and up my legs, and my gloves are not helping my fingertips keep warm. I know what this is going to mean for my Raynaud's. I am trying not to think about the vast depths of the water beneath me or what happens if the ice splinters and breaks. We have to concentrate on where we are walking, as it is hard not to slip. Cath, who tripped and broke her ankle the previous year, is taking extra care. Together we make slow progress.

Later, Cath admits she was as worried as I was. 'I was nervous that we would go through it because I've never walked on ice because you spend your whole life being told not to walk on ice. It's really counterintuitive.'

When we arrive at the site, it is an extraordinary scene that greets us, so strange that my brain struggles trying to take it all in. All around us divers encased in neoprene are slithering out of perfectly equilateral triangles cut deep into the ice. Their dark shapes look like prehistoric beasts emerging from the primordial soup.

In front of us are divers busy getting ready to submerge. One is already in the water with her arms resting on the ice breathing deeply. I know that she has a huge amount of experience, so I am surprised that she seems to be nervous. If she is worried, then I should be very worried.

Because we are diving under ice, we are going to have to swim alone in the dark along the line. To be as safe as we can, there is one person at the start to offer moral support and a dive buddy in the water, shining a torch at the exit as a guide and ready to stage a rescue if necessary.

What we are trying to do is beyond challenging. All my instincts are telling me it is madness. I try to keep as calm as possible.

Cath is flustered before her turn. The wetsuit gymnastics have unsettled her, and she can't get her fins on over her neoprene booties. As she struggles with her equipment, she goes uncharacteristically quiet. Once she is immersed up to her neck, though, the cold calms her down.

Watching her serenity, I begin to panic, overwhelmed by a feeling of dread. I am her dive buddy, I am in charge of her safety, and I don't want her to do it. I am about to reach out to stop her, but it's too late. She is gone.

The next seconds are the longest of my life. Twenty-five in total. My relief at seeing her emerge safely – and her swearing – galvanises me to get in and get on with it.

It is hard to manoeuvre myself into the water; the fins are cumbersome, and I get them tangled in my legs and lanyard. I am prepared for the temperature to take my breath away, but to my surprise I feel OK, my wetsuit is working. It's only my hands, feet and cheeks that feel sharp pain as they freeze.

A Finnish woman is sitting on the edge next to me, dangling her feet, and she says to me: 'My theory on this is, just don't think about it. They have been overthinking it, just get on with it!'

I agree. My rational mind has taken over. I know I can hold my breath for at least a minute and a half. I know that with one breath and fins I can swim for at least 50 metres underwater. So, I know I can do this.

I make sure my lanyard is attached to the safety line, that my torch is working and that I can see through my mask. After a couple of deep breaths, I pull myself under the ice and go for it.

What happens next?

Massive sensory overload. *I am too buoyant. I am being squashed up against the underside of the ice so tightly that I can't swim. There is no air to breathe. It is dark, impossibly dark. I can't see the exit.* A switch clicks on in my brain and I go into survival mode. *I am calm. I can work this out.*

Time expands.

I turn onto my back, pressing my hand against the glassy underside of the ice, and push myself away so I can free my legs and kick.

I register how surprisingly smooth it is. I thought it would be jagged, and my hands are telling me something different. I slide gracefully along, swimming on my back. I am suspended in space, floating without gravity. With my face turned towards the surface, I realise I can see the dim light of Cath's torch filtering through the thick ice, shining on me as she walks above my head. I focus on it and follow its tantalising beam as if it were a lifeline.

Then panic hits; a wave of alarm crashes over me. *When am I going to get there? This is too far! I am running out of air!* I turn over onto my front, facing the depths, eyes struggling to make sense of the gloom. *Why can't I see the lights at the end? Oh my god, I am going to die here under the ice!*

Milliseconds later, I see the unmistakable shape of a person ahead of me, their legs dangling down from the shelf above. I have made it! Done it! I have swum 15 metres under 1 metre of ice in the dark. My first ever freedive outside a pool. As my mouth breaks the surface, I breathe out hard, gasp for air and laugh my head off. It terrified me – but I *loved* it!

I want another go!

I tell the others what I am up to, and I pull myself under again, making my way back to where I came from. This time there is no panic; it is still scary, but an enjoyable kind of scary.

By the time I get out my hands are so frozen I can hardly move them, and my feet are numb, so I find myself hobbling back to the shore. We pile into the wood-fired sauna and then the outdoor jacuzzi to warm ourselves up. We are high on the adrenaline overload, and talk nine to the dozen.

'We are hard but not stupid,' says Cath, 'but I think it was a bit bonkers to just rock up and do our first ice dive in the dark. It was a bit like having a couple of ski lessons on a dry ski slope, and then the first thing you do on snow is go down a black run in the dark. That's how crazy it was!'

She is spot on. It *was* beyond challenging, and potentially foolhardy, but thankfully we are OK.

The next day, we dive again in the daylight. The lake, which is covered in snowfall, is pristine white and the sky a piercing blue. Visibility underwater is only about 3 metres, so we still can't see where we are going, but it is far less alarming. I love finning on my back and touching the air bubbles trapped beneath the surface.

The day after that, and under impossibly pale blue skies, Cath insists I try her favourite sport: ice swimming – or, in my case, ice dipping.

There is a circular pool about 10 metres in diameter cut into the frozen lake. I get to it by gingerly walking down a wooden jetty with a path of snow down the middle. The water is glassy, and I can clearly see the outline of round flat pebbles on the bottom. My eyes are blinded by bright sunshine sparkling off the ripples made by a water fountain in the middle of the pool.

We have been joined by Elina Mäkinen, one of Finland's most famous ice swimmers. She has been doing a photoshoot with Cath. In their swimming costumes in the snow, they look fabulous. As well as setting up their shoot they have put two thermometers into the water, which say 0.3°C and 0.6°C. The rules for ice swimming are the water must be 5°C or less, so this more than qualifies!

Cath has come into her own right now. She is glowing with joy and excitement. This is what she is made for: swimming in freezing temperatures. I can see from the glint in her eye that she is utterly determined to get me in the water

She gets in first and makes it look as easy and as comforting as stepping into a freshly run warm bath. 'Tropical!' she says. I don't believe her!

She then explains how best to get in. 'You need to get your fanny in, then your tits, then your pits. Once your hands are in keep them in. Bits, tits, pits! It's simple: bits, tits and pits. If you are going to swim, Louise, you need to put water on the back of your neck. So, tuck your hair in the back of your bobble hat!'

That's the only thing I am allowed to keep me warm. All I am wearing is a bobble hat and my swimming costume.

I grip tightly onto the metal steps and slowly ease myself in backwards. When my toes hit the surface, the pain is intense. It is so cold, I feel like I am being burned. Cath is right beside me, holding my hand and encouraging me.

'You are going to love it; I know you will! Deep breaths, one step at a time. Bits! Louise, breathe, sing your favourite song. You went in an ice hole in the dark, you can do this.'

At first, I don't understand what she means by bits, tits and pits – but the water inches up my legs, and I do. Ouch, ouch and ouch again. The air rushes out of my lungs. I can only take shallow breaths.

'It's really sore,' I squeal.

'That goes, I promise. Hold my hand and bend down. You need to get your boobs in now. Put your hands in, and keep them in. Smile!'

Her cajoling is so constant and so funny, I do exactly as she says and somehow get my shoulders in. Letting go of the steps, I manage four strokes of breaststroke before I am allowed out.

I scramble up the steps as quickly as my numb hands and feet will let me. My body is in shock. All the blood has rushed to the surface of my skin, I am pink all over and am simultaneously both cold and very warm. I feel like I have undergone an ice baptism.

Cath gets out behind me, still issuing instructions. 'Get a towel round you, get dry and in the warm, don't go in the shower!'

I am tempted to disobey her, but I know I can't, because it is dangerous to warm up too quickly.

Wrapped in towels and dry robes, we laugh uproariously as we head back to the sauna to bring the blood back to where it should be. I can totally see why she loves ice swimming. The rush I have after putting my body through such a shock is heady and invigorating. I can only imagine the feeling after swimming a whole mile in the cold.

I have loved my time with Cath.

Underwater we have been like two mermaids freed from the constraints of gravity, free to push at the edges of our personal boundaries and free from the judgement of others or ourselves.

She is an extraordinary person, who has done extraordinary things. The cold water is her comfort and her strength, and I feel lucky that she has given me a tiny glimpse into her icy world. She may not be happy herself with her body, but what she does is powerful. It inspires other women to have confidence in their shape and size. She has become a compelling role model, encouraging others to change their perceptions and be fearless.

# 4

# Belinda Kirk
## *Overnight Dartmoor Crossing*
### Devon

We all underestimate ourselves, particularly women. People are most limited by their own attitude, their own belief in themselves.

I watch in fright as Belinda's left foot, boot and knee disappear. She is suddenly up to her thigh in a sticky morass of mud and water. My eyes open wide in alarm. I had been fine until that point. So far, our ambitious attempt at a two-day, 58-kilometre Dartmoor crossing from south to north had been fun. But now, I am afraid.

My mind rushes to catastrophic scenarios: *We're both going to get stuck in this bog, miles from anywhere. I'm going to sink too, and no one will know where we are! No one will ever find us!*

My thoughts are exacerbated by the knowledge there is not even a squeak of a mobile phone signal where we are. Added to that, in the four hours we have been walking we have seen only a lone horse rider and a woman out running with her dogs on the moor. No one will see us. No one will come near us. If we sink, we won't be found.

I move quickly to my left using my walking poles to propel me, in a desperate attempt to reach drier ground or find a foothold on a tuffet of grass that will support my weight and keep me out of the water. We don't need both of us stuck in the mud.

Weighed down by her heavy rucksack, Belinda struggles but manages to pull her leg out and get back on her feet. As she does, I make my way gingerly towards her and we agree to head up to our right, away from the marsh where we hope it will be drier because we can see sheep grazing and watching us nonchalantly.

We lost sight of the footpath a while back when we crossed over a small stream, and try as we might, we can't find it. I think we are lost and say so, but Belinda disagrees.

'We are on the right point of the map, it's just that the path isn't here. Maybe it has moved? Or are we just off the path and can't see it because of the bog?'

Our different use of semantics makes me chuckle over the next 48 hours.

I have spent some time on the Moor, but that was many years ago, and I have never walked across it. Nor had the idea even crossed my mind until my companion and guide on this adventure suggested we try. Belinda Kirk is one of the world's most accomplished and well-travelled expedition leaders and lives close by in Exmoor National Park. She has never done a full crossing either, so this is new for both of us.

As we head north over grassy meadows from Ivybridge at the start of our hike, Belinda pulls her safety sheet out and goes through her emergency briefing with me.

High on the list is making sure we don't get bitten by ticks. She hates them and so do I. She tells me they have a nasty habit of finding the warmest places on your body, and that she has had to remove them from some very embarrassing areas. I do *not* want this to happen, so I listen very carefully to her advice about how to avoid it!

'Do not sit on the grass. Find a rock or sit on a coat or a rucksack. Wear trousers and pull your socks over them so they can't get onto your ankles through the gap and crawl up your legs.'

The other thing at the top of her list to watch out for is cows, especially when they have calves. I have always taken care around cows but never worried too much. She changes my perspective forever when she tells me one of her friends was killed by a herd, and another very badly injured. When we see some up ahead scattered across the path, we take a wide berth around them. They watch us placidly and quizzically as if they are wondering why we are bothering to take the long way round.

Belinda's love affair with the outdoors began when she was a child living on Alderney in the Channel Islands. She remembers it fondly. 'When I was aged about seven, I was allowed to go wandering off all day, all over the island, and I found what I thought was a secret garden. That is when I first felt like I was an explorer.'

That love of being outdoors continued when she was a teenager. At the age of 16, when she was going through a difficult time at home and not particularly enjoying school, she was inspired to take part in the Duke of Edinburgh Award scheme. In addition to volunteering, playing sport and learning a new skill, young people are expected to go on an expedition. The teenagers have to carry all their own kit, navigate the route and camp outside, all under their own steam. That expedition helped set the course of her life.

Twenty years later, a friend reminded her about that weekend and just how important it was.

'She remembered vividly how being outside changed me. She said it was like watching a light come on. At the time I didn't have a lot of self-esteem, and doing something completely outside my normal world, going on an expedition in the Brecon Beacons, gave me a real boost. I found, to my surprise, that I was good at something. It gave me a different way of looking at myself. It made me think there is other stuff out there, a big world, bigger than the little world I live in. So, if I feel like I am not good enough here, maybe I can find a place where I am going to be good enough.'

Our great escape from the marsh has really taken it out of me. It must have added an hour or so to our journey, which was already going to be long. Belinda warned me when we set off at 8.30 a.m. that the day would be arduous. We were hoping to walk about 30 kilometres and get as far as Dunnabridge near Dartmeet, and pitch our tents there.

Normally Belinda would plan a walk of that distance in two and a half to three days, but we are both short of time, so she has planned for us to do it in just two. I knew this would be hard, but assumed I would be OK.

Carrying all the equipment is back-breaking, and I realise I've underestimated how much it will deplete my energy levels.

I have followed the kit list she sent me carefully and included everything: a small tent, sleeping bag and mat, a full set of waterproofs, spare clothes, first aid kit, stove with a spare gas canister, water purification tablets, and head torch. Add in the four litres of water she says we must each have and I reckon that my rucksack must weigh about 20 kilos. And I am feeling every single one of them. Belinda's rucksack is even heavier than mine: she is carrying an emergency medical kit too, and her tent is bigger.

The truth is, after about six or seven hours on my feet, I am shattered.

I might be a two-time extreme triathlon finisher, but I am far from my peak fitness. A double dose of COVID and a knee problem have badly affected my training schedule and, unsurprisingly, my endurance levels too. My legs are tired, my hips are aching from the weight of my rucksack and my shoulders feel bruised from the straps pulling and bumping against them.

The military are using Merrivale Range, one of the firing ranges on Dartmoor, for live ammunition training over the next couple of days, so we can't take the most direct trail north, which would take us through Princetown. We are going to have to head east and take a wide berth to stay out of the danger area, adding 10 kilometres or about two hours' walking to our journey.

Our route will take us past Nuns Cross Farm, where Belinda has stayed many times before when leading navigation or wild camping courses. When we reach it, about eight hours into our expedition, Belinda notices how tired I am and says we can stop there and rest a while.

I am not sure I have ever seen such a scary house in my life. It seems to be glaring down the valley, watching our every move as we make our way towards it. As I get closer, it's even more frightening. It looks as if its eyes have been gouged out and bandaged over because all the windows have been boarded up and padlocked. There are iron bars across the shutters on the ground floor, making it impossible for anyone to force an entry. The porch has a white painted front door, which might look welcoming if it didn't have three large bolts pulled across it, fastened with more robust and rusty padlocks. There is no way in – and the truth is, it spooks me so much I wouldn't want to cross its threshold anyway.

Even so, I am delighted to swing my rucksack off my back and dump it by a huge rock. I breathe a massive sigh of relief as I sit down on it and rest. Belinda sees my expression, digs her gas stove out of her rucksack and makes me one of the most delicious cups of tea I have ever drunk. I don't care that it has a distinct flavour of chlorine. I immediately feel better.

'There's nothing quite like a warm drink to cheer you up, especially here in the UK where the weather is often wet and cool. I call it a cup of morale. There's something about the ritual of making a cup of tea. It's like an achievement in a way as well. It's a good opportunity to stop occasionally and reflect on what you have done or set your expectations for the next part.'

As we sip, we both kneel over the Ordnance Survey Map while the house frowns over us, and she shows me that we have a difficult choice to make. Since COVID, many of the wild camping areas have been closed for conservation, and given where we are right now, our choice is limited.

Either we carry on for another three hours and then find somewhere to camp, or we stop in just over an hour. There is no other option.

If we carry on, and chose the tougher option to keep walking tonight, it will mean tomorrow will be more manageable. It will also massively increase the likelihood we will reach our ultimate goal of completing the full south to north crossing.

I am pretty sure that I don't have another three hours in my legs, so I ask Belinda if there are other ways out of the park. There are, but none of them look easy, and I get the distinct impression Belinda will be more than a little disappointed if we don't make it! I will be disappointed too, but right now, I am so exhausted I need options.

I am relieved that we agree we will look for a camp soon. So for one last time today we pick up our rucksacks and load them onto our backs and head past an ancient cross (Siward's Cross). Incongruously, there is a photographer taking pictures of the ancient waymarker that appears in the history books as far back as 1240. It is part of Abbot's Way, a route used by monks to travel across Dartmoor to Tavistock Abbey – and what Belinda optimistically insists is as good as a motorway.

I look at the route, and decide I love our semantic disagreements: She calls it a motorway, I call it a scraggy track. Nevertheless, I am happy to see it cutting through the moorland and meandering over the hills ahead.

Given the restrictions on where we are allowed to stay overnight, there is clearly going to be no camping by a bend in a lazy river under the shelter of trees. We will have to pitch our tents in the middle of the wilderness; the only shelter we will have is what we have carried on our backs.

With that in mind, we head towards the crest of a slight hill covered with scrubby grass and start looking for an open patch that isn't boggy and which has enough flat ground for each of our tents.

Belinda has made camp hundreds of times before. She has camped all over the world – deep in Amazonian rainforests, on African savannahs, while walking across Nicaragua and in China's Desert of Death. Her experience of leading expeditions in the wildernesses of the world is inspiring. I envy these epic adventures and love hearing her stories. She tells me about one of her first research expeditions in Tanzania, where she lived near a crocodile-infested river and was adopted by a troop of wild black-and-white colobus monkeys.

Watching her set up home for the night, I see that she has it down to a fine art. She is incredibly organised and efficient. The priority is to get our tents up.

'If you get your tent up quickly, especially in this country, then if it starts to rain you can keep all your gear dry. The last thing you want is everything wet and soggy.'

So far, we have been lucky with the weather, but the clouds are gathering above us, and it feels like we might get rain. My tent is brand new, bought for the trip, and I have never put it up before – which is potentially very silly because I haven't even checked it has all the poles and pegs. By the time Belinda has all her overnight things ready, I have managed to get only about half my tent up, and she patiently helps me work the rest out.

As we sit cross-legged on our coats to deter the ticks, I devour my surprisingly delicious rehydrated chicken curry and she tells me about her most challenging and dangerous adventure. Ironically, given how much she has travelled, it took place not in some far-flung country but right here in the UK when she and three other women rowed unsupported around Britain. During the 52 gruelling days she skippered the SeaGals, there were occasions when she feared for her life. One of them was trying to cross a busy shipping lane in their tiny rowing boat, which was dwarfed by merchant vessels.

'I have been on expeditions all around the world, but weirdly the most scared I have ever been was right here in Britain. On our coast we have some of the strongest conflicting currents, some of the busiest shipping lanes and complicated tidal systems. When you are in a small boat that doesn't have an engine or a sail, you try and stay away from the coast rather than follow the coastline.

'At Milford Haven, I felt most in danger. We had to get across the shipping lane. It is a bit like a bicycle trying to cross an eight-lane motorway and so we waited for darkness so that we could see the lights of the large ships. It is easier to cross in the dark because you can see what is coming. And then as dusk fell these dolphins started popping up and swimming around us. It was a super pod of dolphins who seemed to know we were scared, and they escorted us across the shipping lane. Incredible.'

Despite moments of terror, Belinda and her crew set a Guinness World Record as the first women to row round Britain. Sir Richard Branson was effusive with his praise: 'Quite the most remarkable achievement carried out by any women alive today. Absolutely magnificent both for mental and physical achievement bar none.'

Although Belinda is effortlessly modest and wears her multiple achievements lightly, I can tell she is very proud when she says Sir Ranulph Fiennes called their experience 'arduous'. From the mouth of the man recognised by Guinness as the world's greatest living explorer, it is a fabulous accolade.

I can only begin to imagine how extraordinary and harsh that journey must have been. All I have managed is one day walking on Dartmoor, and I feel broken. My body is fizzing with the day's exertions and, embarrassingly, I have to zip up my tent at 8.30 p.m. to go to sleep when it is still light. I sleep fitfully and dream of dolphins coming to the rescue.

I wake some hours later, freezing cold and needing a pee. I clamber unsteadily out of my tent and am greeted with an incredible view. Apart from a slight haze of light where Princetown must be, it is almost suffocatingly dark and the constellations above me look like phosphorescence sparkling in the sea. I can't stay to stare at the stars for long though as it is very cold. When I get back inside, I put on every single piece of clothing I have with me, including my woolly hat and my down jacket to keep warm. The only thing I don't have on is my gloves. For once my hands are warm. My sleeping bag feels like it is doing nothing to stop the cold. It's the same one used by my daughters Mia and Scarlett for their Duke of Edinburgh expeditions, and both had complained about it being useless. I feel bad now that I know why.

Belinda has a cold night too and in the morning emerges from her tent sporting a jaunty woolly bobble hat. Her efficiency is a wonder. She manages to pack and have her breakfast cooked and ready before I have even got out of my tent, even though I am doing my absolute best to be as quick as I can.

Despite the shivery night, I feel ready for a long day. We still don't know whether we will make it all the way north, but the thought is unspoken between us that we are going to try.

Our morning goes well. Happily, we are avoiding the showers that had been promised in the forecast and make good progress in the sunshine. Belinda narrowly avoids falling into the river as she gingerly makes her way over the giant stepping stones just south of Dunnabridge.

I am happy because we are on the path, but then we lose it again in the lee of Bellever Tor. I think I have distracted Belinda with too much talking. Rather than retracing our steps, we pick our way through thick gorse, following what might possibly be a track made by wild Dartmoor ponies, cattle or sheep. Our off-road route has an unexpected bonus, and I realise why the animals wander through when I see Belinda reach down and pick something from the vegetation and pop it into her mouth. It is a bilberry, a wild version of a blueberry. I would never have dared eat one without her beside me, afraid that it might be poisonous. It's like an explosion of sharp but sweet flavour in my mouth. We stop and spend a few minutes grazing on them, and laugh when we see our tongues have turned blue.

The unexpected fruit burst is a powerful fuel, and almost before we know it, we reach our first glimpse of civilisation in 24 hours: the small village of Postbridge. We are hoping to refill our water bottles for our onward journey, but what we find is much more exciting: a Post Office store. It has a pillar-box red, old-style telephone box next to it, a carousel stacked with postcards, and – best of all – a blackboard by the front door advertising its wares. Everything from books about Dartmoor to maps, wine, local cider, clotted cream and – top of the list for me – Cornish pasties and a hot cup of tea, which we enjoy sitting side by side on a bench in the sunshine.

Stopping short of our goal yesterday means we have a long 29 kilometres to walk today, which will take us, according to Belinda's calculations, around 10 hours. That's the best-case scenario, if the route is easy. It could be much more than 10 hours if we have to head off-road again, which is more than likely. What's more, right now there's wind and rain.

As we cross the East Dart River and head into the North Moor, Belinda asks me: 'Do you want to try and make it to Belstone?' To my surprise, I am up for it and shout back enthusiastically: 'Yes, definitely!'

It is funny what being in the outdoors can do to you.

Our conversation turns to the thing she is most passionate about, the transformative power of adventure. She has spent years exploring, pushing herself and helping others do the same, and during that time she became fascinated by the way challenges can change people for the better. Her book *Adventure Revolution* tells the stories of the many people she has seen change in fundamental ways because of their experiences of adventure.

Today, Belinda points out that life-changing adventures don't have be on an epic scale. You can find them anywhere. An adventure just needs to test and push you as an individual. It could be anything from a walk down a river to crossing a country; every adventure can make you different.

'Choosing a challenge that you find intimidating can unlock your potential because it shows you, you can do much more than you think you can, you are much more capable than you think you are. That is a huge confidence booster, and it doesn't have to be a huge challenge. We all underestimate ourselves, particularly women. People are most limited by their own attitude, their own belief in themselves. If you can unlock that and embrace some discomfort, you can be more fearless, bolder and build resilience.

'I think there is this feedback loop of accomplishment, and with those feelings of joy and awe you can keep growing. You take those skills, that self-belief and that change in you, to the rest of your life. That is how adventure can be transformational. If you step out of everyday life, do something adventurous, you go back to the other areas of your life – your career, your relationship – as a different person, bringing these gifts with you.'

I wonder wistfully what this walk across the Moor will bring me. Right now, all I can imagine is the after-effects of aching shoulders and blisters on my feet!

Dartmoor is steeped in ancient history; its hills are littered with stone circles that serve as enduring reminders of ancient times. Belinda is determined I won't leave without seeing one and she navigates us with precision to the Grey Wethers stone circles just west of Fernworthy Forest. We sit in the centre of the smaller of the two prehistoric circles, and have our lunch.

Belinda takes out her Ordnance Survey Map again and counts the grids carefully with three fingers to estimate how far we have to go. She reckons we are about 9 kilometres from our final destination. On an easy, flat route that should take three hours, but the going is about to get really tricky again. We will be off-road, and having seen her sunk to above her knees in the mud yesterday, I know what that means. This is going to be hard.

We need to get to the top of Hangingstone Hill, near the perimeter of the military firing range, from where we can follow a track made by off-road vehicles towards Okehampton. The problem is, to get to that part of the route there is no path marked on the map.

As we head east over an ancient clapper bridge across a stream and up the hill towards the ruins of a settlement, it starts getting tough. What is hindering us this time isn't marshland but what from a distance looked like innocuous and lush green grass. Up close, it is something quite different: lethal, ankle-breaking terrain. In some places the grass is as high as my shoulders and has grown in tussocks a foot or so above ground level. You can't stand on the clumps because they aren't stable, so you have to find a foothold beneath them on ground you can't see. At least twice I trip up, with both feet stuck beneath the tangle of vegetation, and end up face-planting to save myself. Funny but also worrying.

Belinda's navigational skills are a wonder to behold. Throughout our whole walk she has constantly been checking her OS map, and her ability to be right almost to the metre and the second is impressive.

I ask her where she has used her skills, and she tells me she has honed them over many years successfully navigating through rainforests where rivers can move, and deserts where dunes can shift, but also mountains where accurate navigation can save your life. She recounts the story of an expedition on Ben Nevis when she was leading a group as the cloud closed in, hiding the path. She had to pace the track to know exactly where they were and to stop anyone falling over the edge.

We have been blessed with perfect visibility on our journey, and as we reach the top of Oke Tor and sit and rest for one last time, we are rewarded with a stunning panoramic view over the hills towards Okehampton. I phone up a taxi and ask them to meet us in the pub in Belstone at 8 p.m. According to Belinda's calculations we should be there by 7.30, so we are leaving ourselves time for a pint, fingers crossed. After nearly 11½ hours on our feet, we round the corner, to be greeted by the welcome sight of a whitewashed pub packed with customers enjoying a meal and a drink. It's 7.29. She is incredible!

I can hardly move. I am exhausted. I feel like I do when I have finished an extreme triathlon: shivery and nauseous, needing to eat and sit down. I tease Belinda, saying that she has broken me! I am only half-joking, and she looks worried as the taxi drops her at the train station for her onward journey and I slump in the back.

And yet, according to Belinda's philosophy, feeling like this is an important part of the adventure.

'It is not an adventure unless there is adversity. If you aren't suffering a bit, and by that, I mean, too hot, too cold, wet, hungry or tired, you haven't left your comfort zone. It is beyond your comfort zone, where you stretch yourself, that you learn. It is visceral. It doesn't mean you have to scare yourself to death, or have a terrible time. It is not about being gung-ho and having to suffer, but about pushing yourself to your edges. Adventure shows you what you are capable of and helps you discover what your physical and psychological boundaries really are.'

As the salt from a big packet of crisps restores my energy, I reflect on the many things Belinda has taught me. What I love most is that she has shown me there is no need to travel abroad to find adventure. It is right here on my own doorstep if I just take the time to step out and explore.

I am inspired. I have an almost brand-new tent and I know I will go back.

# 5

# Zainab (Zee) Alema
*Rugby*

## Richmond Rugby Club

Rugby culture is very alcohol-based. Imagine me, a young Muslim girl ... I am covered up, I don't drink, I am playing rugby. I felt the odds were against me, but I felt I loved the sport.

I am soaked to my skin. Everything is wet – my hair, my bra, my pants. I am dripping. Wet through.

If I stopped and thought for a second, I would probably realise I am cold too, but I don't care, I don't give a hoot. I am running around on a muddy rugby pitch, splashing through puddles lit up by the floodlights soaring high above me. We are playing in the middle of a violent thunderstorm. I am sprinting after the ball, tackling anyone I can catch, forgetting I am 53, not 23. I don't care about the rain or the temperature, or that sometimes it hurts. I have been transported by the joy of competitive sport.

I have been invited to play at Richmond Rugby Club by Zainab (Zee) Alema – or, as she is known on the pitch, the Bulldozer. Her nom de guerre is intimidating, and on the pitch, playing the game she is passionate about, she is a force to be reckoned with. Off the pitch she is a gently spoken neonatal nurse and mother of three young children under five. It is an intoxicating combination, and she is smashing all sorts of stereotypes. She has a burning ambition to be the first Black Muslim woman to play for England.

Richmond Rugby Club is steeped in history. Founded in 1861, it was one of the founding members of the Rugby Football Union, and today, over 160 years later, it has accomplished men's and women's teams. This is where she trains – and as I find out, she trains hard.

It is a short walk from Richmond Underground station, and only two short miles from the home of England Rugby: Twickenham Stadium, where Zee wants to play. The entrance, when I cross a dual carriageway and finally find it, is old-school: a red-brick pavilion with white windows, and a balcony with painted ironwork balustrades. It's like something out of a 1920s' film set. I know it also has a brand-new state of the art stand, but that doesn't draw my attention.

I have never met Zee, but I have been looking forward to doing so since interviewing her on a podcast and bonding over our mutual experiences of Chelsea and Westminster Hospital in London. She worked there as a neonatal nurse in the intensive care unit, where I spent one of the most traumatic weeks of my life. My daughter Mia was born by emergency C-section, and a week later my appendix burst. The medical staff helped to save both of us, and I feel that Zee and I have a shared history.

She is waiting for me outside the entrance to the club. She greets me with an instantly recognisable dazzling smile, and gives me a great big hug. She looks exactly like I have imagined her: strong, and tough. I thought we were the same height, and I am surprised that I am taller.

Even with the warm welcome, I feel out of place and intimidated. This is not my natural environment. I don't know either the actual rules of this game or, even more importantly, the unwritten rules – the customs and habits and responses which come with knowing a sport. It is all alien to me. I have only ever watched rugby on the TV or from the side of the pitch. I have never stepped onto one.

We take a selfie outside the entrance, and I laugh as Zee tells me I must hold the ball. She can't because she is sponsored by Canterbury and this ball has another logo. When she hands it to me, I realise I don't know how to hold it, let alone throw it or catch it. Tonight is going be a steep learning curve.

Zee walks me through the car park, chatting about the books she is planning to write – one a children's book and the other about her journey. Off the pitch she laughs easily; her voice is soft and quiet, and musical.

I am joining her on one of her evening training sessions, ahead of an important match on Sunday. From what I gather over the next couple of hours, the team's confidence is bruised after their last encounter and there is work to do.

The two of us arrive just as a motley crew of teammates make their way to the edge of the pitch, some arriving in cars, some walking, all carrying bags of kit which they dump on the grass before getting changed and putting on their boots. They are all shapes and sizes; it doesn't matter what you look like, there seems to be a place for you. I might fit in. They have a casual ease about them, and the conversation bubbles along. It is a warm and welcoming sound.

Zee introduces me: 'This is Louise, she is going to train with us, and she might join us for the game on Sunday!'

That makes them laugh. I laugh nervously too. I think some of them really think I am considering joining the team. I am embarrassed and admit that tonight is the first time I have ever touched a rugby ball, let alone tried to play the game.

I look around to see what everyone is wearing and am relieved to see I seem to have the appropriate clothes. I am almost wearing the same as Zee: black leggings, long sleeves, and a jumper. She says it might rain later, so I put my rucksack under my waterproof as she hands me a brand-new, bright orange pair of shiny rugby boots. They are incredibly flashy. Someone chuckles and says that if I am going to wear them, I am going to have to play well. Chance would be a fine thing!

As I struggle to tie my boot laces, Zee joins the others on the pitch to practise one of their set pieces. About 10 line up in two parallel rows, one behind each other. I stand to the side, watching, trying to work out what is going on and to decipher their secret codes.

Zee is very calm, very focussed, clearly a key part of the team. I hear her whisper to a teammate: 'Let's go for Gold Strike.'

In response, the ball is thrown in from the sidelines. One person jumps, arms aloft, and in unison Zee and another player grasp her thighs and lift her up effortlessly. She floats high up into the air, as if she was flying, and catches the ball with ease, bringing it down to the ground. As one, they huddle around her, shoulders together pushing forward, a powerful unified force.

Zee leads the shout. 'DRIVE 2, 3, 4! DRIVE 2, 3, 4!'

They sound like a raging army going into battle.

It wasn't an obvious or easy path for Zee to go into rugby, but looking at her now, I see no hint of how hard it has been.

'Rugby is known to be a white, male, middle-class/upper-class sport. When I told my dad I wanted to play rugby, he said: *Why would you want to do that? Rugby is for men; it is an elitist sport.* There are a lot of stereotypes about Muslim women in general: that we stay at home, cooking and cleaning; that we are not allowed out; that we have multiple kids. There are lots of stereotypes, especially in the media, and it makes it hard to be a Muslim woman in this day and age. People don't know what we are about. I am trying to do my bit to change that by telling them my story.'

Her story first started when she was in Year 9, doing a PE session in a school in West London. On what Zee reckons was a bit of a whim, the teacher suggested they try rugby. Everyone apart from her didn't want to play, worried they were going to fall over. By contrast, she thought running into people would be fun.

'I loved it the moment that I touched that ball, and I was running with it. It was amazing.'

A few years later, another teacher suggested she play rugby as part of her practical for A-level PE. Her teacher was determined to find Zee somewhere to play, and not only managed to find her some funding but drove her in her white Nissan Micra to sign up for Ealing Trailfinders.

Zee's passion for the sport continued, and she went on to play at university, where cultural differences nearly made her give up.

'Rugby culture is very alcohol-based. Imagine me, a young Muslim girl who doesn't drink alcohol. I am in uni, I have joined the rugby team, I am covered up, I don't drink, I am playing rugby. I felt the odds were against me, but I felt I loved the sport. The team never made me feel not welcome, but stepping onto the pitch I was conscious I was the only Black girl, the only Muslim girl.

'Then afterwards we would go to the bar. If you were Woman of the Match, which quite often I would be, you would have to down a pint. I would stand at the bar, and I would have to reject a pint because I don't drink. I felt embarrassed having to reject the pint and I would have to nominate someone else to have it. It sounds minor, but those little things played a big role for me and made me almost want to leave the game. I never said anything because I thought: *If I say something I am going to be more of an outcast. I am going to be admitting that I am different from my teammates.'*

What she wears on pitch makes her stand out too. 'I am covered, from my ankles to my wrists, as well as wearing a hijab. My teammates have their beautiful legs out, I look different from them, and that made me feel awkward too.'

Being able to wear her hijab on the pitch was incredibly important to Zee. Around the time when she was considering giving up, there came a seminal moment when she looked up the rules about wearing the hijab. There it was in black and white: she was allowed. Then, she says, she knew that rugby was meant to be; she was meant to continue playing. But wearing a headscarf doesn't come without its problems.

'Rugby is a physical game, and obviously my hijab can come off. When I first started playing in the early days for Ealing, I did have an incident. I was running down the wing and I scored a try, and I was so happy I got up elated and my teammates were not cheering me on and were not happy. I was like, *What is going on?* Then I felt the wind on my scalp and realised. *Oh my God!* My hijab had come off 10 metres away and I didn't even notice. It was so embarrassing because my hair wasn't done! That was the main thing. I was having a bad hair day, and of all days for my headscarf to come off it was that one. I slowly picked it up and put it back on my head. Everyone was like, *Are you OK, Zee? Are you alright?* They were all really concerned, and also shocked, as they had never seen my hair before.'

Since then Zee has always worn a scrum cap over her hijab when playing, and it has never come off again.

Once everyone has arrived, head coach Mark Cadogan calls us towards him to start our warm-up. It is a tough one. Mark barks out instructions and everyone obeys. Putting in maximum effort, we do shuttle runs backwards and forwards between the try line (where the goalposts are) and the 22 metre line. We lunge, sprint, skip, and bear-crawl. I try and copy Zee as best I can but fail.

'Louise, don't let your knees touch the floor. Get your hips below your shoulders. You are not doing yoga!' shouts the coach.

Very quickly I am sweaty and out of breath.

We are told to pair up. Zee chooses me, and we are told to practise lifting and carrying each other. Zee goes first, bending down and clasping her arms around my thighs, lifting me easily off my feet and dropping me down 2 metres away. Her strength and power are impressive. I take my turn. I am convinced there is no way that I am going to be able to lift her off the ground. But Zee talks me through the technique, and tells me to brace my core.

Some final words of encouragement – 'Go for it, Louise!' – and I take a breath, and much to both of our surprise, I lift her off the ground and carry her about 1.2 metres. I feel a massive sense of achievement. So far, so good.

We move on to practise the scrum. This time I can't join in; it would be too dangerous. Zee is involved because she has just moved to a new position on the team as a prop. I know that they are the real toughies on the pitch, the battering rams. The ones right at the front of pretty much everything. She explains her role to me with infinite patience, the way a teacher introduces a new student to something they have never done before.

'I am in the front row. It's a very taxing position usually played by the stronger and bigger players. We have to do everything. We are in all the set pieces, in the scrummage, also in the line-outs. We also carry the ball round the park and do the tackling, and when we have done the hard work, we ship out the ball to the backs, the faster players, and they score the tries.'

She mentions the stronger and bigger players, and I remember that, as a future rugby player, Zee had an inauspicious start.

She was born premature at just 26 weeks, 14 weeks early, and even though she was born at a good weight for her gestation, she was tiny, so small that her mother says she used to fit in the palm of her hand.

That's why she wanted her own career as a neonatal nurse. 'I felt like I wanted to give back to those that kept me alive. If it wasn't for them, I wouldn't be here.'

That tiny baby nestled in her mother's hand is almost impossible to imagine now, she looks so strong, muscular and powerful.

As a prop Zee must train for the scrum. As we head over to the scrum machine, it starts to rain, and I can see dark clouds looming ominously in the gloom. When I get close to the metal structure, it reminds me of something you might find in a dungeon, a medieval instrument of torture.

There's a set of padded stocks, and three people holding onto each other, shoulder to shoulder, shoving their heads between the pads to push. In front, on the ground, is a metal plate. Zee takes up her position on the left side of the scrum machine and binds onto the hooker on her right, who then binds onto the tighthead on her right. I have to stand with three others on the plate, as a counterbalance so that our weight will stop it moving when they push. They steady themselves. Their timing and precision is perfect, and on the command of *Crouch, bind, set!* they slam into the pads with a force that feels like a car crashing into us. The whole machine jolts backwards as they shout in unison: 'Drive, 2, 3, 4. Drive 2, 3, 4.'

It is terrifying.

They go again, and from my vantage point standing above her I can see the focus and the determination in Zee's eyes. She is in the moment, thinking about nothing else. The Bulldozer.

'I love the name. The main reason I like it is that it fits me perfectly. Why? Because what is a bulldozer? It is construction equipment that smashes things and demolishes things, and me, being a Black Muslim woman in rugby, I am smashing stereotypes.

Not only that, being a mother, having a career in the NHS, all of these things are part of my identity, and I am smashing it because people don't expect a mum of three to be playing rugby; don't expect a Muslim woman to be playing rugby; people don't expect a nurse working in the NHS to be playing rugby. So being all of those things means I am smashing stereotypes. *Bulldozer* for me perfectly matches what I am trying to do, what I am about, my identity, so I love it.'

By the time we have finished with the scrum machine, the heavens have opened and the sky has turned a murderous inky black. Thunder is reverberating all around us. We are going to finish the session with touch rugby.

The coach, Mark, shouts out a reminder of the rules. 'Understood?'

I mutter under my breath that I don't think I have understood at all, but we are off. Running, shouting, passing, falling. The rain is torrential. I feel like I am on the deck of a ship rolling out of control in a force 10 gale with water sluicing all over us, and there are constant desperate shouts.

'Back in, back in! Ready, ready! Get up, get up! On me, on me! Move forward, move forwards!'

The incessant screams are punctuated by grunts and thuds as one or other of us takes a tumble into a puddle.

I thought touch rugby would be painless, and that they might take it easy on me as a newbie, but I am afforded no mercy.

Quickly I realise that *touch* doesn't mean *touch*, it means *shove*, *push*, *grab*, *stamp*, and *trip*. I hobble after a particularly vicious encounter; my little toe has been squashed by someone else's boot brought down hard on my foot as they chased me. I am useless, but I *love* it and I watch in admiration as Zee charges, knees bent, shoulders forward, determined to drive the ball forward.

When we stop, I gasp for breath, and we laugh loudly as the rain comes down in sheets. It has been utterly brilliant and so much fun.

The next day my clothes are still soaked, and even my trainers, which I wasn't actually wearing on the pitch, are squelching, but I am still buzzing from the endorphins. It's only when I get out of bed that I realise how hard on my body the evening was. I can hardly walk, my knees hurt, my shoulders hurt, and I hobble down the stairs.

Even as I do, I think about Zee and what she is doing and why it is so important. Old stereotypes may be set against her, but she is living proof that nothing should stop you playing the sport you love. By doing it, and being vocal about it, she is showing the way for others.

'I may not get there, but just by trying I am opening up rugby to a whole different audience of people who are not really interested or never thought that they could be fans of rugby or watch rugby or play rugby. Me playing for England will open the floodgates for other people, Black people, Muslim people, mothers, people that work in the NHS, anything that I represent. Me having that exposure at the top level of rugby will draw more people into the game. That is what I am trying to do.

'I will fight tooth and nail to get that England shirt. I want to try to get people to positively follow their dreams, no matter what obstacles get in their way, I want people to see me and think, *If Zee can get up and say she wants to follow her dreams, then why can't I?* It could be the smallest thing like, *I am going to go out for a run today, I am going to do some exercise today because someone knows what my story is.* That is the dream.'

'That first cap I get, if I get it, is not for me, it is for everybody who didn't fit in, or who felt like they weren't good enough or that they couldn't follow their dreams. So many odds are against me in general, not just from my identity. If I can do it, then anyone can.'

What a powerful message from a fearless woman!

I can't wait until the day she plays for England. When she does, I will sit down and watch her while cradling her favourite tipple, a hot cup of Earl Grey tea.

# 6

# Sophie Storm Roberts

## *Cycling*

## London to Paris

One life, live it. One day I will not be able to
do this. Today is not that day.

We smell the bakery miles before we see it. The unmistakable and
comforting promise of bread, fresh from the oven wafts over us
like a toasty warm blanket.

It is still very early; the sun is struggling to come up and we
are all very cold. I can change gears on my bike only if I look
down and check where my fingers are because I can't feel them.
My feet are numb too, so I don't know if I can put my foot down
safely without it crumbling beneath me. I am worried that if I try
to stop, I will topple over off my bike.

Unlike some of my cycling companions, I have had breakfast,
if you can call a Snickers at 4.30 a.m. breakfast, but I am already
starving and I reckon we have at least an hour to go before our
first official food stop. I don't think I can wait, so when I pass the
welcoming sign of the pastry shop on my right, and see the lights
are on, that it is open, I shout: 'Let's stop!'

All of us skid to a halt. Four of us tumble into the shop and the smiling French lady behind the counter doesn't bat an eyelid as we order, or ask what we are up to, as if it were perfectly normal for a random bunch of British cyclists to walk into her patisserie at 7 a.m. on a Sunday.

The choice is overwhelming. The display cabinet is bursting with delicately arranged petit fours, coffee eclairs, millefeuille, strawberry cream cakes and macaroons – and those are the cakes I can name! They must have been up all night baking.

Despite the vast selection, it is a croissant I am desperate for, and I have never ever eaten such a delicious one in all my life. It will live long in my memory. It is massive, mouth-wateringly buttery, and still warm. I can feel the blood returning to my hands and feet.

We stand inside the entrance, making way for other early customers as we eat our pastries and gently defrost. Our audacious pit stop is infectious: other cyclists behind us stop, all of them too tempted by the sight of our bikes leaned up against the wall to pass by.

We are in Saint-Saëns, 23 miles (37 kilometres) south of Dieppe, and on our way to Paris. Sophie Storm Roberts, a fabulously accomplished endurance athlete and adventurer who has organised the London to Paris 24 hour Sportive cycling challenge, is somewhere up ahead. I have been separated from her because I was near the back of the queue when we got off the ferry in France, and because French Border Control were checking not just passports but also COVID passes, those of us who were last to be let through are about an hour and a half behind the front.

During the excruciating delay, we had to wait outside with our bikes, and all of us tailenders ended up shivering in 4°C. I was wearing every single item of cycling clothing I had in my bag: gloves, cycling leg warmers, windproof jacket and two gilets!

We had assembled some 16 hours or so before, at the start of the 200-mile (322-kilometre) ride outside the Hare and Billet in Blackheath, and then I had been almost too hot. It was a beautiful bright day in April. Spring was in the air, and this was the perfect weather for cycling. We made a funny sight with road bikes and gear scattered chaotically on the lush green grass outside the pub. We were a hive of activity, people packing and repacking, greeting friends, asking advice and occasionally shouting for bits of kit they had forgotten or broken.

I could see Sophie going quietly from group to group, sitting on the ground, chatting to everyone convivially, asking how they were and whether they had come with friends. If they were on their own, she would introduce them to another cyclist so they could cycle together. After 14 times riding London to Paris herself, and eight times organising her own event, she knows how hard it can be, especially if you are on your own.

'The first time I rode London to Paris, it was really, really tough because I had very little biking experience, and I didn't know the people that I was riding with. We did it on Guy Fawkes Night in November and it rained nearly the whole time and we got lost, but that's what kind of makes it an adventure. Now I have done it so many times people think it must be easy, you know, but you still have to cycle 200 miles in 24 hours. It doesn't get easier.'

I am here with a friend and frequent cycling companion, Mimi Anderson. After Sophie has given us both a big hug, she introduces Jemma and Sam, who are sitting on the grass beside us. They have both come alone. I think it takes courage to turn up at an endurance event solo, especially as a woman, and it's a huge credit to both their bravery and to the empowering influence Sophie has on other people. Within a couple of minutes, the four of us decide that we will set off together.

It strikes me, watching Sophie, that she is an adventure evangelist, and her love of pushing herself inspires others to do the same. She is an irresistible force. Where she leads, others follow – and today offers proof. Cyclists have arrived in South London from all over the world to join her.

I first met Sophie a couple of months previously on a walk in the Peak District, which she had organised for International Women's Day. She posted on Instagram to ask if anyone wanted to meet up and hike in Edale. Thinking it would be a great way to interview her and have a mini adventure, I went with my daughter Mia and Labrador Ruby.

When we turned up in the car park next to the station, there were about a dozen or so other women, most of whom had never met Sophie. On that blustery day, somewhere high on the hills, trudging through peaty puddles and being buffeted by the wind, Sophie suggested that I join her for a bigger adventure on the 200-mile ride from London to Paris. So here I am on a Bank Holiday Saturday at the end of April.

Our safety briefing from Chris, the event organiser, makes me think. The number of competitors means that between us we are effectively cycling the circumference of the globe. The inference, which he doesn't actually articulate, is that statistically it would be lucky if one of us isn't injured or doesn't have an accident.

I listen carefully.

'In this kind of event nearly all the accidents happen on hills, usually at the bottom of the hill, where there is a bend. That is because often there is sand or gravel in the road, and when you hit the bend at speed, the wheels go from under you. So, be very, very, very cautious on those hills. Don't be the person who has the accident!'

Sophie is emotional when it is her turn to speak. She stands in front of us smiling brightly, her long blonde hair tied in two unruly plaits escaping from her helmet. She is wearing a blue, red and white event cycling jersey, with a Union Flag on it and the words *London to Paris 24 hour Sportive*, with her motto: *One life, live it. One day I will not be able to do this. Today is not that day.*

Her nails are painted in glittery red, white and blue with the Eiffel Tower on one of them, and *I love Paris* and *I love London* emblazoned on a couple of the others.

The event has been cancelled for two years in a row (COVID, again), so this year feels special, particularly for those who had signed up for the 2020 event – including a couple who met during one challenge, got married and came back to celebrate their tenth wedding anniversary.

As Sophie speaks, her enthusiasm is palpable. 'Two words that spring to mind when I think about London to Paris are *community* and *courage*. This is more of a tribe or a family, that's what you are. Enjoy it, go for it. Everyone is nervous, everyone is thinking: *I wish I had done more training*, but the hardest part is getting here. No one fails on this event. If you come into Paris after 25 hours, or 30 hours, or if you have to spend some time in the support truck, the fact you are here, you are showing up and you are giving it your best and having a go, that in my eyes is a success. That is something you should be proud of, because so few people do it.

'When you get to Paris and then the Eiffel Tower – in the next days, weeks, months and years of your life, remember that courage, that sense of achievement. It's something that no one will ever, ever take from you. For the rest of your life you will remember, *I cycled from London to Paris in 24 hours*. And that is an incredible achievement.'

As motivational speeches go, it is excellent and as we clip into our pedals and head out of London, avoiding buses, cars and pedestrians, the 200 miles ahead don't seem insurmountable.

Our 58-mile (93-kilometre) route to the coast takes us almost directly south through Chislehurst, Westerham, Edenbridge, Maresfield, Uckfield, Glynde and finally into the port at Newhaven, where we are due to be on board the ferry across the Channel by 10 p.m. The pressure is on to make it because, as Sophie puts it, 'The ferry waits for no one!'

Our little group of four – Mimi, Jemma, Sam and I – start towards the back of the pack and make great progress sticking together through South London. They all laugh at me when I have to come to a sudden halt after the light at a pedestrian crossing suddenly turns to red and I shout: 'Trying to stop!'

Thankfully I do, and none of them run into the back of me.

When we start hitting the hills of the North Downs, super-strong Mimi, who has done masses of training, powers ahead, as does Sam. Jemma and I take it in turns to bring up the rear.

I feel good, somewhat surprisingly since I have just had COVID for the second time in three and a half months. Last week there is no way I could have made it up one of the hills, but I seem to have recovered OK.

Sophie had it too, at exactly the same time. 'I haven't been able to do any exercise for three weeks, apart from one big training ride which broke me.' Despite this, there is no doubt that Sophie is a strong rider, and she makes it look effortless, her powerful legs driving her along with hair streaming behind her. She looks like a 21st-century Boudicca conquering the roads in front of her.

We pass through the Kent and East Sussex countryside, with rolling fields of eye-catching yellow oilseed rape, punctuated by dark tunnels of trees with branches hanging over carpets of bluebells. I am captivated by the lilac wisteria hanging off chocolate-box cottages and love whizzing past the Tudor timber-fronted pubs.

The going gets tougher when we get towards the ancient Ashdown Forest and hit a hill that seems to go on forever. I try to distract myself from my screaming thighs by listening to the birdsong as we cycle through the soft light of the woodland. Someone reminds me as we pass Hartfield that we're passing Pooh Corner. That makes me smile.

When we reach the sandy ridge of the High Weald it is turning chilly; the sun is slipping behind the heathland, softening the colours of the gorse and heather to subtle ambers and purples. Up ahead, some of our fellow cyclists have stopped at a Mr Whippy ice-cream van. Sophie is there, smiling as ever and holding a 99 ice cream. The group first met on the ride in 2016 when they all turned up solo, and they have been friends ever since. They even have their own WhatsApp group, Team Ice Cream, and it is now tradition to stop and have a break there.

Sophie's cheery greeting is tempting, but we are all shivery and so opt to carry on.

As we drop down towards the coast, we pass the entrance to Glynde Place, the location for the world-famous Glyndebourne Festival. It is disappointingly quiet tonight; there is no opera echoing over the fields. I would have loved to hear rousing classical music to get me through the last few miles.

We follow a deserted cycle route that turns to the west, directly into the setting sun. We stop for photos and to make sure our lights are working for the last drag into Newhaven. We are cycling in the pitch black as we make our way to the docks to embark on the ferry.

We have a very long wait ahead, and Sophie and I are the best prepared for a sharp drop in temperature. Everyone laughs when I drag out a onesie and a woolly hat from the bottom of my rucksack, but I am toasty and cosy as I sit on the car park tarmac, stretching out my tired legs and waiting for everyone to get through passport control. Sophie comes down the line like a mother hen to check that we are all OK, and I am glad to see that she is wrapped up too, in a bright yellow down jacket and bobble hat.

After some time, we are told to get on our bikes and cycle towards the ferry slip. For some reason – perhaps because I am travelling on my bike and not in a car – I was imagining a small boat, but as we walk up the ramp to the lowest deck, I look up at the bow, open in front of us like the jaws of a giant beast about to swallow us all up, a remake of Jonah and the Whale. Inside we balance our bikes against the bulkhead, where they look small and out of place. I can't really believe that in a few hours' time, all being well, every single one of us will have arrived in Paris on a set of skinny wheels.

Sophie and I are sharing a cabin. We don't have long to rest and neither of us can sleep much.

Sophie has not always been an endurance athlete or sports leader. 'I always did sport when I was at school, but I was never particularly good at it. I was quite overweight, I was uncoordinated and never any good at running. But I loved being active, and I always had the desire in me to challenge myself. I am that stereotype of believing it is the taking part that counts, not the winning, as I never ever came close to winning.

'I was always excited by stories where people would go and do incredible physical feats and face all the elements and overcome all the obstacles that no one thought they could manage. That is what inspired me.'

After university she was working for a tech start-up company and feeling like she was going nowhere. She decided to take on her own challenge and try to triumph in the face of adversity.

'At work the door kept being slammed in my face and I was told to pipe down, sit in my box and just do what I was doing, rather than come up with solutions.'

Things changed for her during a conversation with a mentor, who said: 'A ship in a harbour is safe, but that is not what a ship is built for. Go sailing.'

That famous quotation changed her life.

'It inspired me to think outside the box and the world that I was living in and to just dream for the first time. I thought: *What would I do if I wasn't doing this? What's holding me back? What's stopping me? And what's the worst that can happen? Even if I spend all my savings and have to get another job, that's not really that bad – and, in the process, I might end up learning loads and having an incredible opportunity to create a life I truly love.*'

With those thoughts in mind, she quit her job in 2013 and set off on an extraordinarily challenging expedition to climb the highest mountains in the eight Alpine countries and cycle between them. She is the only person in history to do so – and in 32 days she climbed a distance five times the height of Everest.

The challenges kept on coming. She has climbed Mont Blanc, finished Ironman Wales twice, run 62 miles (100 kilometres) from London to Brighton, and raced her bike across America from coast to coast – among other adventures.

We are having this conversation just shy of 10 years after she reimagined her life. 'I remember mind-mapping all the different things that I love to do and thinking how much I'd love to take people on adventures, but I never really imagined that it would evolve in the way that it has.'

I think about that as I set off some time after her into the dark with my lights on my bike flashing. Bleary eyed, and shivery after the long wait at border control, I lead our small peloton away from the Normandy coast and put my foot down in an attempt at warming up. It is mercifully flat, which means we can get up a bit of speed. No one apart from us is awake. There are no cars on the road, our progress is watched only by cows nursing their calves, and slight horses munching monotonously on scrubby grass. We carefully follow the pink arrows that mark our route.

As the sun comes up, grey mists float gently over the rivers and lakes. The temperature seems to drop even further after the first hesitant rose light of dawn.

Two and a half hours into the ride, and even after my pit stop and the emergency croissant, I am still very cold – so much so that I almost enjoy the effort of the long steep hill on the way into Buchy for our first official stop of the day. Under the timber eaves of the covered market, I grab a cup of tea and fill a baguette with a random assortment of ingredients that I think will keep me going: namely cheese and Nutella. Our gang of four are still together, but it is clear that the delay at the port means we are quite far behind Sophie.

Somewhere past Le Héron, among rolling fields of wheat, our mini peloton has swelled in size and we are now about 12. Behind me is a cyclist who looks out of place in our group: he is a full-on MAMIL (Middle-Aged Man In Lycra), in a red and white skintight cycling jersey paired with matching shorts – unlike the rest of us who are still sporting assorted extra layers for warmth. He tucks in right behind my wheel. I am confused about what he is doing and who he is. When he passes me, I say hello and he answers back in French. I ask what he is up to and François explains he is out for a training ride ahead of Paris-Roubaix, one of the 'monuments' or classic professional cycling races, which he is doing as an amateur. When I tell him we are on our way to Paris, he decides to stick with us – which is lucky because suddenly the pink arrows turn to fluorescent yellow and black, and we are sent off on what seems to be a circuitous detour heading away from our route. But he knows where we are going, and we all follow him, and end up zipping down a fast descent into Les Andelys.

We come round a precipitous hairpin bend, and I catch my first panoramic glimpse of the Seine meandering through a luscious green valley beneath tall white limestone cliffs. I know we are going to cross the mighty river several times before we get to the Eiffel Tower, so it gives me a glimmer of hope I will finish this journey.

At our second checkpoint of the day, we have finally caught up with Sophie and I introduce François. She chats away with him in excellent French before making sure we are all OK and have enough supplies of food and water to keep us going. She is a constant motivator, her words of encouragement pushing us all towards the finish.

Finally, the day starts heating up and the next few miles pass in a blur of sleepy villages and shuttered houses decorated with curtains of cascading wisteria. My French shadow eventually peels off just before Giverny, after over 30 miles (48 kilometres) cycling with us. I told Mimi we would eventually outcycle him!

I keep noticing flower stalls on the roadside in every village and town. I can't tell exactly what it is they are selling, but it looks a bit like the long green leaves and flowers you find on wild garlic. We wonder if perhaps it is Mother's Day. Only later do I find out it is May Day, and they are celebrating in the traditional way by giving each other sprigs of lily of the valley for good luck.

Passing through Giverny on a bike is a sensory experience; the roads are lined with tall poplar trees and the way their leaves deflect the light makes it feel calm and peaceful. The town and its landscape were made famous by the Impressionist painter Claude Monet, and I freewheel as I pass where he lived, standing on my pedals to peek over the stone walls to catch sight of his green-shuttered house.

The ride gets tougher after Giverny. We are making progress, but after nine hours on the road we are all suffering. Behind me I hear Sam saying: 'Everything hurts. I can't sit on my saddle. I think I might faint.'

The last bit rings alarm bells in my head. I know she has run out of fuel, and we need to stop. I know she needs sugar, and she needs it now. It is tricky to stop on an incline, but up ahead I can see a gravel driveway. We turn in and come to a halt.

She has nothing to eat with her, so I give her some of my emergency food. I put my hand on her back and tell her it will be OK. Her recovery is miraculous: from having tears in her eyes, she puts the smile back on her face in less than two minutes, and we are off again. We find Mimi and Jemma waiting at the top for us under the shade of the forest.

Sam is not alone in running out of fuel. Sophie has done the same too.

'I have had moments like that on other events and challenges and on London to Paris. Whenever you feel that tiredness coming on in your legs, it is always food and nutrition. The way that I look at it is that your body is a machine, and you have got to keep this machine moving for 24 hours, so must constantly check in with it, thinking: *Does it need food, does it need water, does it need to stretch, does it need a rest, do I need to put layers on or take them off, do I need a hug or a pep talk?* It's like a constant oiling of a machine, that's how I do it. It is so interesting to learn about your body, and how to navigate and negotiate with your body to be able to do these phenomenal endurance events.'

The culmination of our journey is spectacular, and cycling into Paris feels like a privilege.

I love the series of bridges we cross over as the Seine flows back and forth through the city, the dark water lazily sliding beneath our pedals. We are taken off the main road onto a cycle path through the Bois de Boulogne, a glorious oasis of green populated today by families and friends making the best of the sunshine. We slow down to navigate carefully around other cyclists and walkers out for a Sunday stroll.

I think we must be close to the end when we catch our first glimpse of the superstructure that is the Eiffel Tower, but someone in the pack says we have at least another 8 miles (13 kilometres) to go. I am hoping that isn't true.

On the busy main roads, the Parisian drivers give us a reassuring amount of space, but we seem to be stopped by every single traffic light. It's exhausting and debilitating clipping in and out of our cleats. It also means we keep getting separated from each other, but invariably those in front always wait on the other side. After nearly 200 miles, Mimi, Jemma, Sam and I are inseparable.

Then, to my surprise, we hit more hills. I had no idea there were any hills in Paris. I am feeling slightly delirious, and I fear we are going round in circles.

As we edge closer to the finish, the architecture gets more dramatic. The gothic churches with their spikey spires remind me that this is an ancient city with a rich history. We navigate another bridge. As we ease ourselves around another tricky roundabout, I realise that have lost count of how many we have crossed, and suddenly, ahead of us, towering into the clear blue sky, is the wrought-iron monolith that is the Eiffel Tower. I am dwarfed beneath it; it is breathtaking.

We have to cycle round two sides to reach the finish, avoiding crowds of tourists who are looking up, distracted by the view. It is frustrating and slow, but before I know it I have tears prickling my eyes, making my nose tingle. My daughter Mia and my dad are there waiting for me. I wasn't prepared to be emotional, I hardly ever cry, but, as they give me huge, warm, welcoming hugs, I sob tears of joy and relief.

Sophie has been crying too. 'I think it's just this, like, huge relief, because you finally get it done and your loved ones feel so safe and comforting, after this sort of out-there experience.'

Sophie has been there for an hour or so, greeting every single one of us with a smile and an embrace. Her mum has a bag full of medals which she has been putting around people's necks. I can see how proud Sophie is of us all. I feel proud too.

I know I will always remember the day that I cycled from London to Paris. As Sophie says, the knowledge that I managed to do it will always make me a little bit braver.

'The main reason that I do all these challenges, and I champion them so much, is because it's the part of you that nobody will ever be able to take away from you. For me, I always wanted to be somebody who was strong and resilient in life. And I'm not talking about being physically strong – obviously, that's great – what I mean is, somebody who can survive the storms that life sends me, so when something happens, I know I've got this. I can back myself. When something goes wrong, you've got two choices. You either get knocked down by it and stay down, or you find a way to pick yourself up and keep on going, and ultimately, that is the person that I want to be. So that's what drew me to these challenges. It was a way to be brave in life.'

That night she makes a speech at the celebration dinner, thanking everyone for the part they played. Her decision to throw her life upside down and reinvent herself has paid off – not just for her, but for everyone she encourages to stretch their own boundaries, to become fearless. Watching her,

her eyes shining with both exhaustion and elation, I think what an incredible gift she has: a unique ability to be able to inspire others to test themselves, push themselves and prove themselves. And, for at least that one day spent with her, to live by her motto: *One life, live it!*

# 7

# Mollie Hughes
## *Mountaineering*
### Glencoe

There is something about the allure of Everest that captures and captivates you, and once it does, it kind of gets under your skin.

Mollie reaches down and very precisely touches the highest point of a stack of chunky metamorphic rocks piled precariously on top of each other. They are all different sizes: some are as small as my hand, others are large, too big and too heavy for me to lift. They seem incongruous where they are, somehow out of place. Their uneven geometric edges make it difficult to stand on them and breathe in the staggeringly beautiful view.

It is March and this feels like the first joyful day of spring. Gone are the dark foreboding skies of winter. The air is so clean it feels crisp and sharp in my lungs. I can see in perfect detail snow-dusted hills for miles around me. It is impossibly clear up here, so clear that I feel like I have 20/20 vision.

We are right at the summit of a Scottish mountain, and just one glance at Mollie Hughes tells you she thrives in this kind of environment. You can see from her body language that she is in her happy place. A wide, invigorating smile washes over her face;

she is nonchalantly holding an ice axe in her hands, legs wide and hip to one side. She is not afraid about keeping her balance or falling, even though there is a steep drop just behind her, making me nervous.

The cairn marks the top of Meall a' Bhùiridh. It is one of Scotland's 282 Munros and is set high above Rannoch Moor, squeezed between Glen Etive and Glencoe. Its name translated from Gaelic means 'Hill of the Bellowing', which refers to the majestic red stag that can occasionally be seen meandering across its steep slopes. I hope we will be lucky enough to catch a glimpse of one on our journey today.

I copy Mollie and point my forefinger, attempting to tap the stones the same way she did, thinking it must be a mountaineering superstition to touch the pinnacle when you get to the summit. She laughs and points at the tip of another rock on what I think must be a man-made pile and says: 'I think that one is higher.'

As she leans over to show me, I can picture her doing exactly that on the summit of Everest – except there she wouldn't be sporting just a T-shirt and lightweight trousers, with her curly blonde hair scraped back from her face. At the top of the world's highest mountain, she would be looking and, I imagine, feeling very different. The temperature on Everest is always well below zero, sometimes as low as -30°C. At the summit, most of her face would be covered by an oxygen mask and she would be dressed in a big down suit, like a sleeping bag but with arms, legs and a hood, and carrying a bulky rucksack. As I cast my eyes over the spectacular but low peaks surrounding us, I ask her to describe what she saw from 8849 metres.

'The view is incredible, absolutely incredible. You can look out and see the curvature of the earth; you can see the whole of the Himalayas sprawled out beneath you. On one side is the whole of

Tibet and on the other side is the whole of Nepal. You can see for miles and miles.'

Mollie is a very accomplished mountaineer; she has been on top of the world not just once but twice. She first climbed the world's tallest peak at the age of just 21. I find that hard to imagine. She would have been the same age as my daughter Mia is right now and I would be terrified at the thought of her tackling such a treacherous feat at such a young age. I don't say this out loud, but Mollie echoes my thoughts.

'That first time, at the age of 21, as much as I felt like an adult I definitely wasn't.'

Not content with summiting once, Mollie climbed Everest again a few years later, the second time from the even more challenging north side of the mountain. She became the first English woman to summit from both the north and south, and in doing so she broke the world record for being the youngest woman to climb both sides. Nor is that her only world record: in 2020 she broke the record for being the youngest woman to ski solo from the coast of Antarctica to the South Pole.

She is one of only 678 women in the world who have ever managed to climb Everest. I am fascinated by her tenacity, and I have been looking forward to spending some time with her in her favourite environment.

We first meet in the car park of the Clachaig Inn, where I have chosen to stay because it is steeped in history, including my own.

The pub is a couple of miles off the main road, nestling in the majestic mountains of Glencoe and dwarfed by their scale. The austere, white-washed building with a steeply pitched granite roof and small windows looks haughty and unwelcoming, but I know it is a safe place for travellers like me. It is said to be the birthplace of Scottish mountaineering, and climbers and walkers have been staying there for over 300 years.

The hotel is right at the bottom of the Aonach Eagach ridge, the dramatic location of one of the most notorious hillwalking challenges in Scotland. The path along it is extremely dangerous. In some parts of it there are 900-metre, sheer drops.

For Mollie, safety is priority No. 1. She arrives with Stevie Boyle, a colleague and friend – and a mountaineering guide with 20 years' experience. I know I am going to be looked after.

Today is going to be all about learning snow skills. The first thing Mollie teaches me is how to attach my crampons. These are 2.5 centimetre/1 inch-long metal spikes on a frame that attaches to the bottom of mountaineering boots. Mollie and Stevie are meticulous in their explanation of how to attach them, making sure I have both buckles on the outside of my ankles, that there are no creases in the strapping and that they are nice and tight. Wearing them will mean I will be able to dig into the snow and ice safely on steep, slippery slopes.

Stevie explains how to walk. 'You need a slightly wider gait, so you don't stand on your boots or your trousers and kick yourself on the back of the ankle. Think about always being hip-width apart. It should feel a bit awkward. It is kind of like you are strutting around.'

He laughs when I say it sounds to me like a walking version of manspreading.

They hand me an ice axe, which again looks lethal. At the top of the 30-centimetre metal handle is a spike on one side (the pick) and a spade-like edge on the other (the adze). It might look like a dangerous weapon, but it could save my life.

'You always hold it in your hand which is facing up the mountain, the uphill hand. Do *not* hold it like a handbag, hold it with purpose. Have the bit that looks like a spade facing forwards. If you fall and start sliding, you need both hands on it and you need to roll onto it. Dig into the snow using your weight and look away from the spike with your feet up. If you remember nothing, just remember to have both hands on it!'

As I head towards the ski lift carrying my extra bits of kit, I ask when hiking becomes mountaineering, and Mollie says it is when you put your crampons on and use an ice axe. I like the simplicity of the definition.

To make it easier for ourselves and to get to the snowline quickly, we catch the chairlift up the mountain. I know that hopping on and off without skis to slide on is going to be hair-raising. My timing has to be perfect so I can put my feet down at exactly the right moment and run out of the path of the chair before it bashes me on the back of the knees and brings me down. Mollie instructs me on how to do it and together we jump, land safely and get out of the way.

Within a few minutes of walking, we reach the first splattering of snow. This is what we are here to explore. It feels more like ice than snow, granular and slushy. It is crunchy like sugar and doesn't have the feathery lightness of freshly fallen flakes. I fiddle inexpertly with the crampons. They are awkward and confusing to get on, but this is what I am here for: the mountaineering has begun.

Being a mountaineer was not something Mollie had ever dreamed of when she was growing up. 'When I was about 10 my brother was 12, we were in Wales and he and my dad were planning to climb Snowdon, and they invited me. My mum was going to the spa, and I was like, *Why would I want to go and climb the mountain in the snow when I could go to the spa?* And that is what I did. I went to the spa.'

As we make our way up the side of the slope, the snow gets deeper, not so heavy under our feet. We are sinking into it. Hollows of springy heather trying to escape from its icy clutches appear like purple pockets. Apart from that, it is pristine. Nobody but us has been here since the last snowfall.

As I trudge behind her, our conversation almost drowned out by the scrunch of our boots, I ask her how she changed, in only a few short years, to a person who decided to climb the world's highest mountain.

As a teenager she had done some hiking as part of the Duke of Edinburgh Awards, and also conquered the Ten Tors in Dartmoor. Things moved up a gear when she was 17 and went on an expedition to Africa. There she climbed Mount Kenya. This was her first experience of altitude, and she loved it. That was quickly followed by another trekking trip to Ladakh in Northern India, and then tackling some very challenging volcanos that are part of the Andes, near Quito in Ecuador.

Everest first came onto her radar when she was at the University of the West of England, in Bristol. She was trying to choose a focus for her dissertation for her degree in Psychology with Sports Biology. Mollie is dyslexic, which creates difficulties, so she knew she had to choose a subject that would keep her motivated. The one thing she knew she was passionate about was mountaineering and so she tried to find a way to link that to her studies. She asked herself, *What is one of the most psychologically challenging mountains?* The obvious answer was, of course, Everest.

'There is something about the allure of Everest that captures and captivates you. Once it does, it kind of gets under your skin. Once you think maybe you could do it, that feeling is hard to get rid of.'

Having decided she wanted to study the psychology involved in climbing Everest, she interviewed seven men who had conquered the mountain. Much to her frustration, she failed to find any women willing to be interviewed.

After speaking to all her interviewees, she found there was a constant that ran through their experiences: a deep emotional attachment to the mountain. Their passion was so infectious that by the time she had written up her findings, Mollie had also fallen under its spell. Their enthusiasm eventually persuaded her to try and climb the mountain herself, even though she knew it was an undertaking fraught with jeopardy.

And, beside the physical dangers, there were other pressures: the worry about the strain on her family and friends, the massive effort not just to train for the mountain but also to raise the money needed to get her there. In her search for sponsorship, both her age and the fact that she was a woman counted against her.

'As a woman, if you get yourself to the final stage with a company, in a fancy boardroom asking for £50,000, and they look at you and compare you to the other person looking for sponsorship – who is a big bloke, with a beard, who might be ex-military – they think: *Who are we going to trust with our money?* They presume he is more likely to get to the top – *He will make it and we are guaranteed our PR* – so they choose him. The irony is, because of the age I first climbed it, I got much more press and PR.'

I'll probably sound naïve, but before Mollie pointed this out, it hadn't occurred to me that one of the many reasons only 8 per cent of those climbing Everest are women is those type of barriers and the discrimination they face right from the get-go. It's no surprise that one of the private sponsors who has supported Mollie through most of her challenges is a woman, who met her after listening to her speak.

'She came up to me afterwards and said, "I want to support you in what you are doing." She is a really great woman who wanted to see me achieve. Her support has been incredible.'

One of the most surprising of Mollie's concerns ahead of Everest was a fear of heights. Her first experience was a tough one. 'As cool as it was to get to the top, it was kind of traumatic.'

She doesn't elaborate just yet because we are short of breath. Trudging our way up the hillside is extremely tiring. I have fallen into step behind Mollie and Stevie. Even with my crampons the snow is sapping my energy, and it is easier to follow in their footsteps than to try to make my own path. Our progress is slow, so we stop for a break, and perch on the rocks.

There is no breeze at all. We can't see anyone else. It is quiet, and peaceful. We are overlooking the bleak expanse of Rannoch Moor stretched out below us. I can just make out the road, hugging the side of Loch Ba. The peaty water of its tributaries is burnished silver in reflected sunshine; a delicate blue haze is blurring the outline of the hills. I am so used to rushing or racing that I am unaccustomed to this steady, measured pace, and I am enjoying it.

As we sit and snack on Snickers, Mollie explains speed is not a priority when it comes to tackling mountains. 'Expedition mentality is about self-preservation, about getting there slowly and safely. Extreme sport is about mental resilience, not about being fast or first. It is about being in the outdoors and part of it.'

She takes me back to what happened on Everest, and her story is not what I had expected. It started even before she got to Base Camp. On her first Himalayan training expedition, she was climbing an infamously challenging technical mountain, Ama Dablam, and there was a fatality. One of the mountaineers fell while abseiling. Many years later, it is obvious that the impact has lasted.

'I think what happened made me a safer mountaineer for the rest of my career. I don't do a lot of things because I don't feel I need to.'

Compared to Ama Dablam, Everest is significantly less challenging. 'Everest is not a technically hard climb, as it has fixed ropes which are set all the way along by the Sherpas, so you have to be competent with crampons and ice axe. You don't need Alpine climbing skills apart from knowing how to

Escaping from Alcatraz with incredible long-distance swimmers Mitali and Anaya Khanzode. They are only 20 and 17 and have braved the leap from the ferry into San Francisco Bay over 75 times each. Just after I splashed into the choppy waters behind them, I felt something brush against my leg...

*'I think once you have swum Alcatraz you have earned a lot of bragging rights. There is something iconic about its shock value.'*

Minutes before our jump you can see our nervous excitement as the notorious island of Alcatraz and its infamous prison loom behind us.

Credit: Christine Grosart.

*Above*: Wild caving terrified me! This is a rare moment of calm with my breathing under control, deep below the Chiltern Hills, as I take in the beautiful colours of the prehistoric rocks.

*Left*: The huge smile on my face tells you how glad I am to be above ground again with wild caver and expedition leader Christine Grosart. She is one of a kind, and has explored places no other humans have ever been.

*Below*: Guinness World Record holder and ice-swimmer Cath Pendleton was the first female to swim a mile inside the Antarctic Polar Circle. She is an inspiration to reluctant swimmers and clearly in her element in the freezing temperatures ahead of our freedive under ice in Finland.

Freediving under the ice in the dark is the stuff of nightmares. There is nothing quite as alarming as the moments before I took a deep breath and hauled myself into the freezing water.

*'We're both going to get stuck in this bog, miles from anywhere...'*

Explorer Belinda Kirk's passion is the outdoors and the power of adventure to change lives. She has led expeditions all over the world and took me on an epically challenging two-day hike across Dartmoor, where I thought we would be lost forever in a swamp.

Credit: Ian Stone.

*'I will fight tooth and nail to get that England shirt.'*

Zee Alema is a force to be reckoned with. Known on the pitch as the Bulldozer, she is a neo-natal nurse and mother of three whose ambition is to be the first Black Muslim woman to play rugby for England. She taught me how to play for the first time at Richmond Rugby Club, and I now understand why she loves the sport so much.

'For the rest of your life you will remember, I cycled London to Paris in 24 hours, and that is an incredible achievement.'

What a brilliant message from adventure athlete Sophie Storm Roberts when she greeted me as I arrived on my bike in Paris.

Feeling like I am on top of the world in Glencoe with mountaineer Mollie Hughes, the youngest woman to summit Everest from both sides.

Concentrating hard and wearing spiky metal crampons to stop me slipping on treacherous spring snow above Rannoch Moor. I felt safest when I followed Mollie's experienced footsteps exactly.

Not all heroes win races: I share Caroline Bramwell's triumph as she finishes a tough triathlon second last, with a stoma.

*Top*: Diving into a new world, mountain swimming in Snowdonia (Eryri) and experiencing the life-enhancing freedom and ethereal beauty of cold clear water. This felt like a seminal moment for me after leaving my job on *BBC Breakfast*.

*Right*: Wrapped up warm after my sublime swim with Vivienne Rickman, mountain swimmer and gifted underwater photographer.

*Bottom left*: Laughing before dawn on the top of a hill in the Yorkshire Dales with Ironman champion and oncologist Lucy Gossage. This was the start of an exhausting 16-hour day of hiking, mountain biking and paddleboarding. We managed to laugh all the way to the end!

*Bottom right*: Surprising myself by managing to stay on my bike while descending tricky mountain trails near Pateley Bridge.

Credit: Jan Kirkham.

*'She seems to be part of the bike, melded to it, perfectly in tune with it, like liquid mercury moving around the track.'*

Reunited with my *I'm a Celebrity... Get Me Out of Here* co-star, the legendary gold medal-winning para-cyclist Kadeena Cox in her happy place, a velodrome. We first met in a cold castle in North Wales where we were living off rice and beans and having cockroaches thrown over us, hence the relief you can see in our hug.

Loving being put through my paces by Kadeena on the track at Lee Valley VeloPark, and dreaming of having a tenth of her power and speed.

Credit: Jan Kirkham.

Smiles before the clouds descended on the Pyg Path on Snowdon (Yr Wyddfa) with charity fundraiser extraordinaire Rhian Mannings.

Frozen at the summit of Snowdon (Yr Wyddfa). Rhian is holding the teddy in the centre, and I am in red on the left waving. I was so cold and wet, I thought I was on a fast-track to having hypothermia.

*'Mimi reminds us to celebrate our bodies not for what they look like but for what they enable us to do.'*

Basking in the sunshine cycling from Chile to Argentina with record-breaking endurance runner-turned-cyclist Mimi Anderson. She is the most infectiously positive person I have ever met, and we were never more than two metres away from each other for the whole of the bike ride.

Staring into the distance in the safety truck at the end of day 8 of our journey across Argentina. I am so exhausted I can't even eat my ice cream and am watching in admiration as Mimi still manages to chat despite the miles in our legs.

Credit: James Appleton.

*'I go as fast as I dare...'*

All alone in the Andes, and holding onto my brakes for dear life. This is the mind-blowing descent from the Chilean Border at over 3,800 metres high, towards the lush valleys of Argentina.

Credit: James Appleton.

Cleaning up the River Trent with Lizzie Carr, intrepid environmental campaigner and standup paddleboarding world record holder.

Roped up and ready to ascend the wall at the Castle Climbing Centre in North London with para-climber and disability campaigner Anoushé Husain.

Enjoying spring sunshine in the Peak District with game changer Rhiane Fatinikun, who set up Black Girls Hike to challenge the lack of representation in the outdoors. We were joined on our hike by my loyal Labrador, Ruby.

Smiles and miles. The one and only run I managed for the book because of a persistent knee injury. Joyous jogging around Thorney Island with legendary endurance runner and cancer survivor Susie Chan.

look after yourself in cold weather. But the heights are tricky. On the south side you have to cross these horrible crevasses on ladders with crampons on, and you have to balance on metal rungs on the ladders with a massive 50-metre drop beneath you. And it is terrifying. The year I climbed, a Sherpa died in one of the crevasses, and we had to pass the place it happened on the way down. I could see the smear of blood on the side. It was six months after my friend had died on the other mountain.'

Mollie's first ascent of Everest truly unsettled her. 'We got up early and summited before most people because it is so busy, but on the way down at the Hillary Step, we met the queues of people coming up and got stuck, unable to get down and past them, and I ran out of oxygen.'

To be trapped at 8000 metres above sea level is life-threatening. There is a good reason this is called the death zone; the oxygen is so thin at that altitude humans cannot survive for long.

'Because I had been off the oxygen for a while, I got quite sick on the way down. I had frostbite in my finger, and I got tracheitis – the lining of my trachea deep within my airway was inflamed. I was a mess coming down, coughing my head off the whole way.'

The mountain didn't just challenge her physically, it also challenged her psychologically. 'After the expedition, I felt a bit unbalanced. I had put so much into thinking about Everest, planning it. I thought there must be more to it than that?'

It would have been easy to say, *Been there, done that. I did what I set out to do, I climbed Everest* – and leave it. But Mollie felt she had unfinished business.

'A year later, when I had forgotten the pain, I started thinking *Maybe I will go back, and this time try the north side*, which is more remote and isolated. That felt like a proper mountaineering expedition rather than queueing in a line to get to the top. It was a much happier experience; we had a much smaller team making our own decisions. For me it is about the journey, about being part of the environment and absorbing it, not just about getting to the top.'

Before she left to tackle the north side, Mollie had an inkling that she might be the first English woman to successfully conquer both sides of Everest. What she didn't know was that she would become the youngest woman *ever* to summit both sides.

As we set off again, Mollie gently chides me for not carrying my ice axe properly.

'It is not a handbag, don't swing it! Make sure you always have it in your uphill hand and that you plant it in properly so that it will hold you if you slip. Plant it and move towards it, so it is always in the snow.'

I realise I am going to have to concentrate on my coordination. I am used to using walking poles, and the axe feels too short for me even though it isn't. To plant it with precision I have to lean down towards the slope, which is really steep now, about 40°, and the last thing I want to do is to fall and slide down the hill. I persevere, and by the time I can see the welcome sight of the summit I have found a rhythm, swapping hands successfully when we traverse and change direction.

We might not be at the top of Everest, but the view from where we are is breathtaking.

It is a stunning spring day, one that makes me want to shout out loud to celebrate the end of winter. We have been extraordinarily lucky with weather: the sky is a hazy pale blue and the few clouds there are above us are decorating it like delicate meringues tipped with white icing. At the summit we can see for 360° around us. Behind us are the peaks of Creise, and the stunning northeast ridge of Stob a' Ghlais Choire. They are Munros too and are covered in a patchwork quilt of snow draped haphazardly over the rocks and scree. In the far distance we can make out the flat top of Ben Nevis and its sheer face falling off to the right-hand side.

I feel like I am on the top of the world at only 1108 metres.

As we stand taking in the surroundings and the sunshine, Mollie tells me how lucky we are. It is only the second time this winter season that she has been out in the hills without being dressed from head to toe in waterproofs, hood down, braced against the wind, not stopping for breaks or even lunch.

As we head back down the mountainside, ice axes in hand and taking care to keep out of the way of the spring skiers, I ask her about her second World Record. In January 2020 she became the youngest woman in the world to ski solo from the edge of the Antarctic continent to the South Pole, an environment so inhospitable that not even bacteria can survive.

It was an epic journey, one that pushed her to the edge of human endurance. To survive on her own with no support she had to be incredibly disciplined, spending two hours every morning and every evening putting her tent up or taking it down, melting snow, drinking, eating, packing and preparing. When she was skiing, dragging her heavy sledge with all her kit behind her, she would listen to music on repeat, and when she didn't, her brain would go into a sleep-like state and she would spend hours going over long-forgotten memories. I find it strangely calming just hearing her description.

The expedition started well, but then, a couple of weeks in, she was hit by a massive weather front with storm-force winds and a complete white-out. Her only option was to hunker down and wait it out in her flimsy tent for two days, with only her own thoughts for company.

'I was really cross with myself because I wasn't making any progress. It was then I decided I had to be really nice to myself in order to be there. You must be your own best teammate if you have no other teammates because you just get frustrated at how slow you are or that you're running out of food. There is no point, you have to find solutions. After the storm was quite a dark phase where I was really behind schedule, exhausted from pulling the 100-kilo sled. It was like I had a black cloud on my head. So, I had to get rid of that, and I realised I had to be nice to myself.'

She remembered a TED Talk and a conversation with someone about the power of positive affirmations.

'At the time I thought I would never look in the mirror and do that, but I was so desperate I tried it. I chose three phrases. The first one I would say was *I am stro*ng, because at the time I felt so weak. So, I said the opposite of what I felt. The second was *I am inspiring people.* That was so important because it was just too hard for it to be solely about my achievements. And the third wasn't about how I felt, but how I wanted to feel. I would say, *I am a fucking badass!* And that was the most powerful. At the start I would whisper them, by the end I was shouting them. It worked almost immediately, as I started laughing, and I hadn't laughed since I last saw another person. After three or four days I felt like myself again.'

The affirmations worked, and after 58 long days alone Mollie reached the Geographic South Pole, becoming the youngest woman in the world to have achieved the trek solo. One of the people who greet explorers arriving at the South Pole said to her she was one of the sanest people they had ever seen coming off the back of a two-month expedition. She laughs at that thought and describes it as one of the biggest compliments she has ever been given.

Since returning, Mollie has become the first female to be President of the Scouts in Scotland. I can't think of a better role model for all the girls who want to get into the outdoors and explore for themselves. With her as a shining example of fearless tenacity and steadfast determination, I hope that the next time a young woman appears in a boardroom looking for sponsorship for an expedition, she will have an equal chance of getting it.

# 8

# Caroline Bramwell
## *Long Course Triathlon*
## The Cotswolds

I say this to people in business as well: *If
I can do it, what is your excuse?*

Triathlon is a hard sport.

I have done dozens of triathlons in my life, and all have
been challenging. From my first sprint triathlon in 2013, when I
panicked while swimming, to Patagonman, where I jumped off
a ferry in the dark, they have all been tough. Every triathlon I
have ever done has pushed my limits and brought moments of
excruciating pain – but a bit like childbirth, I somehow forget
how tough they are and delete the agony from my memory
bank.

Until now, that is. Right now, I am remembering it all and
seriously reconsidering my choices. I am six hours into a middle-
distance race, or what you might call a half Ironman. I am in pain.
A lot of pain. My hips are going into a spasm, and my thoughts are
worse. The negative part of my brain is operating on overdrive.
Telling me: *I can't do it! I don't need to do it. I can stop. I am
going to stop. I don't need to carry on. I won't. I am injured.
I am stupid.*

Somehow, and right now I don't know how, I have to find a way to persuade myself to keep moving for another 10 kilometres and finish a half marathon.

Do I feel up to it?

No.

And yet, I'm not here alone. Playing on a loop in my mind is the story of the woman I am accompanying. Yes, I am in pain, but she must be too. And this is a second challenge she's taken on, to add to her first.

And as far as I know she is not wimping out.

I am in the heart of the Cotswolds accompanying Caroline Bramwell, who is doing this same triathlon with a stoma.

Not only does she have a serious health condition but she also knows that it is more than likely she will be one of the last people, if not the very last, to complete what is a very long course. To me that takes a particular type of bravery.

'Everything I do is to show people with a stoma that you don't have to stay at home. It is not an excuse. I say this to people in business as well: *If I can do it, what is your excuse?* I think we can all do it; it is like mind over matter.'

'A stoma,' as Caroline explains, 'is where the end of my intestine comes out through the wall of my abdomen, and I have to stick a stoma bag on top of that protrusion to collect the output, or what you might call faeces. I had to have an ileostomy because I had ulcerative colitis.

'Colitis is an autoimmune disorder where your system thinks that you are the virus. It is as if your body is attacking itself, and that causes ulceration of your intestine.'

In her book *Loo Rolls to Lycra* (Pitch Publishing, 2018), she explains in graphic detail the devastating impact. By the time she had the operation she could be no further away than 1 metre from a toilet and was effectively housebound. Doctors tried to keep her symptoms under control with steroids, but even with constant treatment she had to be hospitalised and received two blood transfusions.

She made the difficult choice to have a stoma because of her two children. 'I was becoming an invisible mum. I couldn't do anything. I couldn't even get down on the ground to play with the children, because it would trigger an attack and I would have to rush to the toilet. One of the biggest reasons I opted to have surgery was so that I could have quality time with the kids. Had I not had surgery, it could have been life-threatening. If it had gone on uncontrolled, ultimately I could have ended up in a coffin.'

It is a sobering thought, and right now, it's keeping me moving on the run course. My current predicament is my choice.

I first met Caroline in 2017 when she had just taken up triathlon and we were at a charity dinner: the Golden Thread Ball, hosted by para triathlete World Champion and star of *Strictly Come Dancing* Lauren Steadman. It was a 1920s theme and we were both wearing flapper dresses à la *The Great Gatsby* along with glittery headbands.

Today, before we begin, the pair of us couldn't look more different. Neither of us is wearing a stitch of make-up, Caroline has dyed her short dark hair a plum colour and mine is tied up in a scruffy ponytail. We are both wearing tri-suits and loaded with triathlon paraphernalia, including matching pink HUUB rucksacks.

It is a struggle to wheel our bikes through a field over the wet grass and we are late for registration. We would both normally be very agitated by that, but the organisers are relaxed and laid-back, so we are too (more or less).

We spot a toilet, and Caroline very wisely makes us stop. We both know there is likely to be a queue for the portaloos. This seems like an appropriate moment to ask her how she is going to cope with her stoma for the day.

She explains that her preparation began in the early hours. As soon as she woke up, she ate a bowl of porridge and a banana.

I did exactly the same: porridge is perfect fuel for any triathlete because of its slow digestion time. It's particularly good for Caroline because it slows the transit of the food through her digestive system, which is especially important ahead of the swim. After breakfast, before she gets in the water, she takes a couple of Imodium tablets. These are normally used to treat diarrhoea, and mean that when she is swimming her 'output' (her word) stops. She will take another when she gets on the bike.

I ask her if she has to change her stoma bag on the bike. She tells me that she has never had to do so in a race, and though she has had to stop to go to the loo and drain her bag, she has always managed to do that in a toilet and not out in the countryside.

Right from the start we know this is going to be a tough day. It is raining as we rack our bikes, so unless we are careful all our kit for the bike and the run is going to get wet. I did my last triathlon a year and a half ago, and I am struggling to remember where to put everything.

Caroline is incredibly organised. She arrived a day before me to recce the bike course and look at the lake where we will be swimming. The medical complications of managing a stoma mean that, except for the swim, she carries her medical supplies with her all the time.

'I carry more stuff than most people. In my little pot on the bike I have a couple of spare stoma bags and white disposable bags to put them in if I need to do a quick change. Then for the run, particularly a long one, I wear a bumbag with all my medical kit.'

At the lake we know that we are in the final wave of the swim and don't rush too much. Caroline knows that swimming is not her forté!

'I get really anxious before I get in the water. I can get really panicky and hyperventilate if I am not feeling calm. So, before the race starts, I always like to do a bit of a warm-up if I get the opportunity.'

Out of the 600 or so athletes, we are almost last into the lake and walk side by side down to the water's edge, fiddling with our goggles and hats. The water feels warm compared to the chilly air; it is surprisingly clear and feels soft on my hands. As I swim, I see reeds floating gently beneath me; they look ethereal and calm me down. I settle into a steady rhythm, and concentrate on catching up swimmers in front of me.

Caroline enjoys the swim too, even though she finishes behind everyone else. 'I loved the swim,' she says later, 'considering I was someone who gets nervy when I get in the water. I was immediately comfortable . . . and it was brilliant. I went straight into swim mode. I would say that swim was my most enjoyable ever, and by the time I got to the finish I had my own escort. I had the standup paddleboards, kayaks and a canoe, and a motorised boat was out there too.'

The bike is much tougher than the swim for both of us. The temperature has dropped since we started, and I take an age to wriggle out of my wetsuit. It's a right faff and I take 10 minutes in transition. Caroline takes a little longer than I do.

My hands and feet are frozen from the moment I get on my bike, and don't unfreeze for the duration of the 90-kilometre ride.

The course is psychologically challenging: two laps of 45 kilometres.

The roads are mostly flat, which should be good for me, but I find it hard because it has a series of sections where you go out and then back on yourself. That means you can see other competitors, who are either behind or ahead of you; for some reason, I find that demoralising. In addition, I have to stop for a pee in a field, and by the time I have taken off all my layers of clothes and have put them back on again I have wasted at least 10 minutes. That is followed by another two minutes trying to dislodge the mud which has clogged up my cleats so much I can't get them back into the pedals. I make a mental note to never again go for a pee in a muddy field! And then I remember what Caroline has to manage.

She is out on the course cycling for 45 minutes or so longer than I am. 'The bike was pretty gruesome,' she told me later. 'It was relentless. On the second lap it got windier, and again I had my own personal police escort. I had a motorcycle rider with me at the back, and when we came into transition they put a bike in front of me too, so I felt like the Queen.'

I passed Caroline just once on the other side of the road on her bike. She looked compact and strong. We shouted hello and waved enthusiastically – but it was the last I saw of her for many hours.

As I reach the dismount line, after nearly three hours, 45 minutes of almost constantly cycling, my feet are numb. I am careful to put my leg down precisely, to avoid tumbling over.

From where I saw her on the bike course, I work out that Caroline is quite a bit behind me, an hour or so. *What am I going to do?* I had been adamant that I was not going to run, wasn't going to finish the triathlon – not with an injured knee. BUT! There is always a but with me, especially when there is a medal involved, and these medals are *huge*.

I set off walking, deciding to walk and run. One minute on, one minute off – and, given how slowly I am going, I'm confident that Caroline will catch me.

The run takes us on a three-lap course which for the most part follows the edge of Lake 32. Its prosaic name doesn't do it justice: it is beautiful and tranquil, and the water is surrounded by dense forest and narrow woodland paths. Two or three times on the 7-kilometre loop, you come back on yourself. This means that we can see the other runners running towards us, and I am hoping that means I will see Caroline.

It goes OK-ish for the first lap.

On the second lap things change, and I begin to seize up. I hurt all over, and not seeing Caroline is depleting my determination. *Should I wait? Should I stop? Can I make it round another lap? Is she OK?*

I have a stern word with myself: *I might have a sore knee and be undertrained, but Caroline is doing this with a stoma! Get over yourself, Louise!* Or, as one of my best friends says when facing tough times, *Suck it up girlfriend!*

Caroline tells me later she has a much more positive way of talking to herself.

'I found myself talking to myself out on the bike today. Things like *Come on, Caroline, you can do this. Come on, Piston,* I tell my bike, *we can get up this bloody hill!*'

She has not always been this way, and reminds me she did no sport at all before her ileostomy. 'Before my operation I was never sporty. I would never have done anything like this. The operation transformed my life; it gave me my life back. Some people say the worst-case scenario is that you end up with a stoma – but for me a stoma has been a positive life-changer. It gave me my freedom back; it enabled me to do things with the children again.

'Once that happened, I started to think I need to prove I am in control and prove to others that they can do things. If I hadn't been ill, being a triathlete would never have crossed my mind. I call it PTG: post-traumatic growth. I think when people have been close to the edge, they suddenly see, actually, I'm here for a reason or life has got to be lived. For me, it's like a post-traumatic growth.'

Out there, on the run, I need a serious dose of Caroline's resilience. I am about to pack it all in, and then I am saved by Karley.

In a bright orange running top, she reminds me of an angel who has been Tangoed. Overtaking me for the second time, she stops and says: 'I know you! You are Caroline's friend. I am a friend of hers too. I know her from Ilfracombe. I had cake with her yesterday for my birthday.'

'Yes, I am,' I say, delighted that someone will talk to me. I feel very lonely with my negative thoughts, and ask her: 'Can you help? I think Caroline is behind me, and I don't know whether to stop at the end of this lap and wait for her or to carry on?'

'Stop? What do you mean stop?' Thank goodness, Karley is having none of my defeatist attitude. 'You are not stopping. You are way more than halfway. You can't stop now. I will stay with you and talk to you.'

Running is my least favourite part of any triathlon. I have always felt I do it under duress, just so I can complete the race and get a medal. I will do almost anything for a medal!

In the weeks before the triathlon I had not been able to run at all because it irritated my already inflamed knee and made it even more painful. But not being able to run made me realise something fundamental: I hate *not* being able to run more than I hate running. Sounds weird, but it's true. I really miss it. Yes, I go out walking with the dogs often, so very often I am outside in the fresh air. Yes, I do lots of other exercise, but nothing quite gives me the same buzz as running – even if it's my least favourite part of a triathlon. It is Caroline's too.

'Running is my most horrible discipline. I don't enjoy it because I am not good at it, and I am not as consistent with my running training as I am with my cycling or swimming. That's why I struggle. But my mind is strong; my mind tells me I can do it. I have always had a run–walk strategy; I have always done that, and I always will. I start with four minutes running and one minute walking and will take it down to two to one, or just one to one if I have to. But my mindset will not let me give up.

'I think if we let those demons creep up on our minds, we would give up on a lot more that we ought to. The only thing that has made me stop in races is cut-off times. Even in an Ironman, when I know I am getting close to a cut-off time on the bike and I have run out of time, I would rather they stopped me than I quit. I will keep going until I am told I must stop.'

Her determination is a wonder to behold. Her ultimate goal is to complete a full Ironman distance race, double what we have done today, to inspire other people who have a stoma. In her two attempts so far, at Ironman Bolton, her dream has been thwarted by the relentless hills. As she says, she is 'no skinny minny racing snake', and she didn't manage to make the cut-off time. She was taken off the course, but she has not given up: completing an Ironman continues to be her goal. Next time, she says, she will pick a race that has a terrain that suits her better and is much flatter. I don't doubt that one day she will succeed.

I have been with Karley for nearly an hour now and there is still no sign of Caroline. I am not worried – she is experienced and resilient – I am just wondering where she might be. The paths are getting increasingly empty as other runners pass us and finish ahead of us; there can't be many of us left out here.

I start asking the volunteers around the course if anyone has seen her, but no one has. So I am mightily relieved when, towards the end of my third lap, I catch sight of someone ahead in the far distance running in a grey cap with an Ironman logo and a distinctive long-sleeved pale blue and navy trisuit. As we get closer, I can see Caroline's smiling face. She is looking serene and in control. We stop for a hug and a brief chat, and she tells me she is on her second lap and is going to keep going. I am staggered: she has already been out on the course for about seven hours, she probably has another two to go, and not for one second is she contemplating stopping. I am in awe.

It is a subdued atmosphere at the finish while I am waiting for Caroline. I sit exhausted on a tree trunk, eating a banana and watching volunteers take down the marquees, pack away the merchandise and pick up the last bits of triathlon detritus strewn on the ground.

I always think that this is when the real heroes of triathlon finish. Not the winners, who have long gone home to recover. But the backmarkers, the stragglers who have had the longest day, and the biggest struggles.

Finally I hear news that Caroline has a pacemaker, and they are making slow but steady progress. I can see only three lonely bikes left in transition, which means, since one is mine, that it is only her and one other person out on the course.

Finally, nine arduous hours and 36 minutes since we stepped into the water together, Caroline runs up the soggy red carpet under the finishing arch, and with a broad smile raises her arms in triumph.

She has bloody done it!

She is sparkling with excitement and pride.

I am excited for her – and inspired. As we pick up our bikes and push them back to our cars, the only ones left in the field, I know I will always remember her when times are tough and I'm haunted by moments of self-doubt.

Today she has shown me that, when you set your mind to things, almost anything is possible.

# 9

# Lucy Gossage
## *Team Hike Bike and Paddleboard*
### Yorkshire Dales

In races, when it is hurting, I can remind myself how lucky I am to have a body that I can push enough to make it hurt. I am able to choose to suffer and choose how long I suffer for. It is a privilege.

My mouth is watering.

There is a scrumptious sight in front of me: a steaming hot pancake folded into a neat triangle, with a scoop of vanilla ice cream melting satisfyingly on the side. Decorating the plate is an artistic swoop of chocolate sauce. I can see that the pancake is packed not only with bananas but also with Nutella, which is seeping temptingly out of the sides. It looks delicious and is exactly what my wildest imagination had been conjuring up over the last few hours.

The delicious, sugar-loaded treat couldn't have been further from what I had imagined I would be eating today, when I woke up at 4 a.m. in my tent, achy from the cold. I had spent the night tossing and turning, trying in vain to get comfortable and stay warm. I had hardly slept a wink and I wasn't helped by the incessant snoring emanating from the tents surrounding me.

As I pick up my knife and fork and dive into my unexpected snack, my companions do the same and we laugh. None of us would have believed that 10 hours deep into a very challenging endurance event, and with the prospect of several more hours to go, we would stop for a bite to eat. But it is perfect.

We are not racing; we are having fun and have spent most of the day sharing ideas and putting the world to rights while attempting a very unusual triathlon. It is a Hike/Bike/Paddle, to raise money for the Youth Adventure Trust. The race consists of an 18-kilometre self-navigated trek over the Yorkshire Dales, a 56-kilometre bike ride, both on- and off-road, and a 2-kilometre team paddle on a giant, inflatable, standup paddleboard.

Our team of four may not be fast, especially now we have chosen to have a minibreak mid-race, but we are fearsome. I am surrounded by some very impressive women. First up is Belinda Kirk, expedition leader and adventurer, who invited me to join her on today's fundraising event when we did our epic walk across Dartmoor. Sitting to the left of her is another expedition leader, Jo Bradshaw. She has a very impressive mountaineering CV, and as well as climbing Everest is on her way to conquering the seven highest peaks on the seven continents. At the time I write this, she has summited six. Next to me, beaming like the Cheshire Cat and talking nine to the dozen, is a world-class athlete, and one of the women who inspired me to write this book, Lucy Gossage.

I first met Lucy over four years ago in a tiny town nestled in the majestic mountains of southern Chile. On that day, I heard her before I saw her. Her raucous laugh rippled infectiously across a cavernous sports hall where she was lining up, like me and about 120 other hardy triathletes, to register for an extreme triathlon called Patagonman. My first impression was that she was a gregarious giggler, the type of person who is always the heart and soul of the party. Her laughter is infectious, and startling. The bellowing power of it belies her stature: she is only 1.6 metres (5' 4"), lithe as a whippet and just as fast. On that day in Patagonia, the race number she had been allocated was 1. That tells you a lot about who she is. She was expected to win – and sure enough she did.

Lucy has an intimidating reputation as an athlete. In the world of long-distance triathlon, she is a superstar – one of the most successful triathletes on the planet and winner of an incredible number of tough races. When I first met her, she was the five-time UK Ironman champion, with 12 Ironman wins under her tiny tribelt, and had finished twice in the Top 10 at the legendary Ironman world championships in Kona.

Those results are impressive on their own, but one of the most remarkable things about Lucy is that she won the majority of those races at the same time as working as a cancer doctor. She had to squeeze in her training, and racing, around long shifts working in a hospital, taking challenging medical exams to qualify as a consultant oncologist specialising in the treatment of testicular cancer and sarcoma.

Lucy never set out to be one of the world's most successful endurance athletes. It all started by accident, with a drunken dare.

She wasn't very sporty at school and, aged 13, was ashamed to come last in a cross-country race. The first time she dipped her toe in the world of triathlon was at the age of 26. It was the London Triathlon in 2005, a standard-distance race with a 1500-metre swim, a 40-kilometre bike and a 10-kilometre run. When she entered the race, she was, in her own words, a party-loving, slightly overweight junior doctor having issues with a long-term boyfriend and wanting a bit of a challenge.

She loved it and still has a video of herself running towards the finish line. She describes herself as 'quite big and waddling, but with an amazing grin on my face'.

She couldn't have looked more different when she turned up today, at 5.16 a.m. precisely, just eight minutes ahead of our start time at the Yorkshire Dales Sailing Club on Grimwith Reservoir. She hasn't camped like us because, true to her style, she was working until late yesterday on an awayday with the charity she helps to lead, Move Charity, which helps young people with cancer to exercise. She is living life as she loves it, juggling work and sport.

She is a whirlwind of energy, smiling as ever. Lean, wiry and strong. You only need to glance at her in her bright blue T-shirt, shorts and running backpack, and you can see she has the strength and attitude of a serious athlete. Lucy looks like she was born to race, but the transition from what she called the waddling runner to podium winner wasn't instantaneous.

'A while after that first race, some medical students I was teaching told me about Ironman races. I just thought *What a ridiculous, impossible thing to do!* But a few weeks later, having just been dumped by my long-term boyfriend and commiserating with a few drinks in the early hours of the morning in a nightclub, I dared myself and said that if I was still single on New Year's Day, I would sign up for one.'

A few weeks later at the close of the year, she was indeed still single. That evening she met a man who had done an Ironman. This seemed to her like fate intervening. 'So, the next day I signed up for Ironman UK.'

Taking on an Ironman is a massive commitment. If you have ever trained for a marathon, you will know it takes a huge amount of dedication and focus: months of training, endless long runs, and weekends ruined. The marathon is just one third of an Ironman, so add to that the pressure of training for a 3.8-kilometre open water swim and a 180-kilometre bike ride, and you get an idea of the gruelling nature of preparing for a race that long.

Her friend, who she now affectionately calls Ironman Geek, tried to persuade her that she would have to get out on her bike rather than ride on a spin bike in the gym, and also follow some sort of structured plan. She didn't. For her bike training, she would take the map from her car, rip out a page and use a highlighter to mark out a route that she would try to follow, invariably getting lost and adding miles and hours on to her day.

Her long runs on a Sunday were done mostly with a hangover. 'After partying and drinking until 2 a.m., I would get up and run for two hours without eating any breakfast and would often have to stop to be sick halfway round.'

To say she was underprepared is putting it lightly – and ahead of that first race she admits she was terrified. 'I didn't have a clue, and I honestly didn't believe I could do it. I didn't think I could finish.'

But once again, on race day itself, she absolutely loved every second of the 11.5 hours, especially the finish. 'I was so proud when I crossed the finish line, I felt like I had achieved the impossible. It exceeded all my expectations, and is something that will always stay with me. It means as much and was as emotionally changing as winning races later on.'

When she turned up exhausted for her 9 a.m. shift in the hospital the next morning, that was it, she assumed. She had done it, and would never do another race ever again. She went back to the pub and her busy social life, but something about the experience stayed with her. Finally she realised she missed the exercise.

The transformation to serious athlete happened when she moved from Nottingham to Cambridge in 2009 to start a PhD.

While she was researching, she had to stop seeing patients, and that lack of face-to-face contact had a big impact. She stopped enjoying her work and turned to sport for mental support. She started training, as opposed to just exercising, as a way to validate her days. From that moment, her strength and speed rose exponentially and she started winning races.

She was so fast that in 2011 she took a huge leap into the world of triathlon and decided to work part-time as a medic so that she could race as a professional triathlete, competing for money and not just for fun. It was a leap of faith to invest in her passion, but she was right to trust her gut feeling. Two days after she went part-time, she won her first professional race – and after that kept on winning.

Today winning is not on the agenda. We are here for the chat!

In the triathlons where Lucy and I have both competed before today, Patagonman and Norseman, she came first. I finished a full five hours after her. Normally, the only time I ever see her is at the start of the swim. As soon as we get near our bikes, I haven't a hope of keeping up with her, not even for a minute! She is a machine. That's why I have deliberately asked her to join me in a team event where we all have to stick together.

As the four of us set off, into the darkness, picking out the tricky path across the hillside with the flickering lights from our head torches, it is clear today is going to be all about the banter. You can probably hear us for miles around as we make our way up the narrow windy track that zigzags up a steep hill towards the giant gritstone boulders which mark Simon's Seat, the summit of Barden Fell. Lucy leads the way as quick and sure-footed as a mountain goat. I like to think that I am slow because I am in recovery; it is only eight weeks since I had a knee operation. But I know that if she didn't have to stay with us, light-footed Lucy would have run up the mountainside, leaving us all behind.

It is dawn by the time we get to the top, and we stop for a breather to take in the expansive view – and smile because far in the distance is a glorious, golden shaft of sunshine breaking through the clouds.

As we descend, I'm even slower. My knee is sore, objecting to the downhill pressure. To distract me and make it easier, Lucy tells me about her latest madcap challenges. She has now given up competitive sport and taken up what I would describe as adventure sport.

'It is not about speed any more, it is about personal challenge. I still find ways to put myself out of my comfort zone without a race number on my back.'

She tells me she has taken up cycle touring and biked almost every long-distance gravel route there is in the UK. This summer, just for fun, she and her partner ran one of the most gruelling trails in the world, the Dragon's Back. Over six days they covered more than 370 kilometres, climbing the equivalent of Everest twice on wild mountain paths from Conwy Castle in North Wales to Cardiff Castle in South Wales. I know she is unimaginably tough, but it nearly broke even her.

When I ask her why she chooses to put herself through what seems like hell on her days off, she explains: 'My definition of adventure is something that you think of, and you are really excited about it, and then the night before you think, *Why am I doing this? I can't do this! It is stupid, I want to pull out!* And then you do it and you go through dark patches, and you have highs and lows. But at the end you think: *Wow, that was amazing.* To get the epic highs you have to go through the tough bits.'

Like today, coming pretty much straight from work to join us early in the morning, Lucy has always juggled her work with exercise. She has found that being an athlete has helped her to be a better doctor – and being a doctor has helped her be a better athlete.

.g in oncology, it is really easy to appreciate how lucky
.. I would drag myself on these runs on the ring road in
dark, and my first thought would be *I just want to be lying
on the sofa eating dinner.* I would then think about someone I
had just seen in hospital who is dying, and I think I am so lucky
to have this body that allows me to do this. I think in races, when
it is hurting, I can remind myself how lucky I am to have a body
that I can push enough to make it hurt. I am able to choose to
suffer and choose how long I suffer for. It is a privilege. Cancer
patients don't get that choice. That knowledge is really powerful.'

Her job is almost unimaginably stressful, and exercise has
helped her to navigate sometimes heart-breaking conversations.
'When my head is churning after telling someone that they are
dying, exercise allows me to process that. It is a vital mental
release.'

When Lucy was racing competitively, that unique sense of
perspective was a powerful force, giving her an edge over her
fellow triathletes. She won more races when she was working as
a part-time doctor than in the two years she competed as a full-
time athlete.

What she says makes me reflect on my own experience of
work and sport. The comparison is trivial, but I felt a huge
amount of pressure when I was presenting *BBC Breakfast* in
front of an audience of six million people. I look back, and
sometimes it seems extraordinary that I was at my fastest as
a triathlete and competing internationally for the GB Team in
my age group when I was getting up at 3.40 a.m. for work.
But I knew at the time that the hours I spent training let my
mind have a space to rest; I could process the stress of being
on live television for three and a quarter hours every day, and
the constant fear that at any moment I could mess up. Without
doubt, it was the antidote which helped me cope both mentally
and physically.

We are so distracted by our chatter that the four of us have entirely forgotten that we are in a race. We have been ambling at a snail's pace and are almost back where we started at the reservoir when we are jolted back to reality by the sight of volunteers waving by the flags ahead of us. They remind us what we are supposed to be doing, and we speed up into transition.

Lucy might not be racing competitively anymore but she is still enviably strong, and it is on the bike ride that she comes into her own.

Today's cycle is both on- and off-road, and we have been advised to ride mountain bikes. I don't have one, nor does Belinda, so we have hired a couple for the day. In the race safety briefing we were warned that there were a couple of so-called 'technical sections' where we need to take extra care. I don't even know what that means because I have never ridden a mountain bike on an actual mountain. I wasn't that worried until I sent Lucy the navigation files for the ride. Two minutes later, she sent back a simple message: 'That route is super hilly.'

I looked at the other two. 'If Lucy says it is hilly,' I said, 'then it is going to be a shocker!'

It turns out, I'm right. It's a monumental ride which gets gnarly after about five minutes. I can see people on the steep road ahead of me pushing their bikes.

Lucy takes it in her stride, and as she pulls away from us, shouts back: 'Go at your own pace – it will be easier that way.'

I watch her as she makes it look easy, tapping it out to the top, light on her pedals. I struggle behind her. I am in my easiest gear, determined not to get off. Belinda, who hasn't ridden a bike properly for decades, is struggling too. It is arduous, and I rely on all my reserves to keep turning the pedals. Lucy stops at the top to wait for us under a sign which proves why it has been so hard.

*Long, steep descent*, it says. *Cyclists, check brakes and ride carefully.*

There is also a red triangular warning sign that the gradient is 16 per cent. No wonder my heart is racing!

The route heads off-road onto an agricultural track, which takes us through vast fields towards Gouthwaite Reservoir. I soon learn what *technical* means: a vertiginous descent on a cobbled road littered by huge uneven rocks. It is terrifying. Lucy tells me what to do: keep my knees bent to absorb the shock, place my weight over my back wheel and keep my arms and elbows nice and relaxed. It is so scary, though, I am tempted to get off my bike and walk. The only thing stopping me is knowing how painful my knee was walking downhill. I have no option but to stay on and hope for the best. At the bottom I find Lucy beaming up at us, amazed that despite our inexperience we have all managed to get down safely.

So far, the ride has been brutal – and we don't know it, but there is much worse to come.

The only thing that gets me through the next three and a quarter hours is that seed of hope – and rebellion – planted by Lucy when we turned sharp left in Pateley Bridge. As we whizzed along the flat road, next to the glassy water of the reservoir, she described in glorious detail the delicious plate of waffles she had once eaten in a café there, and suggested it might be a good idea to pop in on the way back.

I never would have dared to stop in the middle of an event, nor would I ever have imagined that Lucy Gossage, legendary Ironman Champion, would make the suggestion, but it feels so brilliantly naughty, all four of us have been fantasising about it ever since.

That promise of food is what I focus on as I battle the most ridiculous climb that I have ever faced on a bike. When Lucy said there was a hill ahead, I refused to believe that we would be attempting to ascend the road rearing up intimidatingly in front of us. I could see a car stuttering up it, engine revving. Surely, the route wouldn't take us there!

I now know Trapping Hill is legendary for cyclists – for lots of reasons. It is an utterly unrelenting 3.2-kilometre climb with an elevation of 262 metres. It has a gradient of between 8 and 20 per cent on some parts and was one of the main climbs of the Tour de Yorkshire in 2017. For the non-technical among us, that basically means it is *very* steep and *very* long. And where we are placed, at the tail end of the race, it also means that most people are not on their bikes. They are pushing.

Ignorance is bliss. When I set off, I have no idea how long the hill is, nor how bad it is going to get, and I am utterly determined I am going to cycle it. Very quickly I realise the only way I can do it is in 50-metre sections. I zigzag across the road to even out the gradient and head for a vaguely flat piece of road where I can stop, breathe and then wobble terrifyingly to get back on. If I time it right, which I don't always manage, I can start pedalling again. I soon realise the best place to stop is where there are piles of road salt on the edge of the tarmac, for de-icing the road in winter. They provide a series of tiny platforms where I can turn my bike around on the gravel and start my next 50-metre effort. It is exhausting, and I am not much faster than everyone pushing their bikes. To get to the top takes me 45 minutes.

Lucy reached the summit about 20 minutes before I did, and by the time I am near, she has given up waiting and is on her way back down to see if we are OK.

The view at the checkpoint is almost worth the effort. We can see for miles. The sun is shining, and the aquamarine sky is interrupted by scattered clouds hanging low. We are elated as we head towards the shimmering water of the reservoir stretching out below us, and the promise of pancakes!

The effect of the pancakes on Lucy is hilarious. On her own Lucy is stronger than the rest of us added together. She has been a constant source of positive energy, cajoling us into carrying on when I was beginning to think we couldn't. And as we head out of Pateley Bridge, she is hit by a sugar rush and her encouragement steps up a gear.

She starts shouting: 'When I say *hard*, you say *core*! When I say *hard*, you say *core*.'

It doesn't take much for all of us to join in.

'Hard!'

'CORE!'

'Hard!'

'CORE!

'Hard!'

'CORE!'

Our responses echo around the valley.

Things finally get easier when we get back to our original climb at Dribble Bridge, and this time we are going *down* the hill with its 16 per cent gradient, not up. The fact that I am a few kilos heavier than Lucy suddenly starts playing to my advantage. I can catch her on the downhill stretches. We laugh hysterically as we zoom along side by side, heads tucked in, trying to be as aerodynamic as we can.

We breathe a collective sigh of relief as we ride over the final rise and cycle into the Sailing Club. The ride is over.

Now comes the standup paddle part of the race, which I have been dreading.

We've already been out on the course for 12 hours, and I am worried we are going to take another two to finish – and it is beginning to get cold. What I hadn't realised was how fast we would be as a team, all of us paddling in unison.

We wobble precariously as we clamber on the giant board. I take up my position sitting at the front because I can't put pressure on my sore knee. The others kneel behind me. We take our directions from Belinda who, with a Guinness World Record for rowing round Britain, is more than qualified to instruct us, and to my surprise we slip into an easy rhythm. We sing our way around the 2 kilometres as the sun sinks below the horizon. We are all singing out of tune and different songs, but it feels joyous and life-enhancing to be with these women, working on the water as a tight-knit team. I can't think of another time when I have had the privilege to spend the day with such a strong, resilient and funny group of women.

It reminds me how much strength there is in female friendship, and how, by working together, supporting each other, you can overcome what might appear to be impossible challenges. One of the reasons I finally won my bruising equal pay battle at work was because I had a strong group of fearless women standing beside me. Together we made the difference.

We mess up our exit and end up having to negotiate a very tricky manoeuvre, backing up our paddleboard onto the muddy shoreline. Once we have stumbled off, we cross the finish line, a full 13 hours after we started and still laughing.

This is one of Lucy's slowest races ever. With us she was never going to make the podium, but our effort doesn't go without reward. We are given a spot prize, for the best reversing on a paddleboard while singing.

Every time I wear the orange beanie hat we were presented with, I will remember this fabulous day and be thankful to Lucy for slowing down and sticking with us to tell me her story. Her joy for life is infectious.

I go home determined to Be More Lucy and to remember that juggling is not always struggling, and that sport is a powerful medicine. I am in agony the next day – pretty much everything hurts – but I am buzzing too, from the exertion and the life-enhancing sense of camaraderie.

I catch up with Lucy a couple of weeks later, and love that even she admits to feeling the effects of our endeavours. 'The next day I set off on a half marathon trail in the hills, and I thought quite arrogantly, *I didn't push myself yesterday, so I will be fine.* I wasn't. I was absolutely knackered!'

I laugh again, glad to know that Lucy is human after all!

# 10

# Vivienne Rickman
## *Mountain Swimming*
## Snowdonia (Eryri)

The scariest thing in the lake is my ginormous magnified body.

I am frozen, shivering violently, shoulders hunched up to my ears, wearing all the clothes I have with me – two coats, woolly hat, socks, boots and gloves. My hands are wrapped around my second cup of coffee and I am sipping it as fast as I dare to, trying not to burn my throat. Huddled in the back of a VW Transporter that has been converted into a camper van, I am sitting on a pile of cosy warm sheepskin rugs, desperately trying to get back the feeling in my body after an extraordinarily serene experience.

I have been mountain swimming with one of the calmest souls I have ever met. Vivienne Rickman is a wild swimmer and talented fine artist whose photographs of women swimming in cold, dark, peaty water are as beautiful and sensual as a Rubens. I have been struck by them for months, fascinated by the colours, movement, tenderness and vulnerability of the images. I love how her photographs celebrate the female form.

I love open water swimming and am passionate about passing on my enthusiasm to others, but struggle to explain why it is so special, and to describe the mesmeric way it affects me. That is why I want to meet Vivienne, because there is something about her photographs which communicate its purity and serenity in a way I can't.

Wild swimming is not a new thing for Vivienne. She hasn't taken it up like so many of us as a result of lockdown; it was passed down from her mother. Her mum was brought up on the Orkney Islands, where there were no swimming pools, so if you wanted to swim, you did it outside. She loved it so much she swam all through the year – which, as Vivienne says, was very unusual in the 1950s. Wild swimming was what they did as a family, on beaches, in streams, in gravel pits. Swimming was part of her heritage, and she was good at it; she went on to swim at club level five times a week. Her mum aspired for her to be some sort of championship swimmer, but as soon as she was old enough to have her own interests, at about the age of 15, she gave up.

I did exactly the same. I stopped swimming competitively from one day to the next because of the way it made me look. At the time, I was a very good swimmer. I loved everything about it, the training and the racing, but one day I looked in the mirror and noticed my muscly shoulders. Very sadly I came to the conclusion they made me look too masculine. I wish I could go back and tell my younger self to be proud and to continue. It took me 30 years to come back to competitive sport – a huge personal loss, from both a physical and mental health point of view.

Vivienne and I are not alone in quitting. The statistics around girls giving up sport when they are teenagers are horrendous.

I was delighted when Vivienne didn't hesitate to say yes after I contacted her, out of the blue, to ask if she would swim with me.

Now, though, I am feeling a little anxious, with a nervous tickle in my stomach as I drive through low cloud, wipers swiping the windscreen, on a miserable day in mid-August, into the dark hills of Snowdonia – or Eryri as it is now called.

The first thing she asked me to tell her – on email, before we even met – was my next of kin. Danger wasn't quite what I was expecting. She added that she would normally ask people about their swimming abilities and experiences, and hasn't done so only because one of her friends watches *BBC Breakfast* and knows that I am a good swimmer. It makes me chuckle, that my swimming reputation precedes me.

She then listed her instructions, which I have obeyed, packing warm clothes, hat, waterproofs, boots, swim kit and a flask. I am worried about the temperature. It is only 16°C outside – and will be much colder in the water. What concerns me is that in all the photographs I have ever seen of her swimming, she is wearing only a costume; there is no wetsuit in sight. I shiver even at the thought, knowing that having Raynaud's syndrome means my hands and feet will go numb after only a couple of minutes in cold water, so feeling like a bit of a wimp that morning I pack my wetsuit as well. I don't know if she disapproves, like some skins swimmers – purists who think that wearing a wetsuit is wrong.

When I meet her in the car park, Vivienne looks like a Viking warrior – tall, strong and powerful. She describes herself as always being a sturdy kind of a girl, but she does herself a disservice: she is incredibly striking. With her long blonde hair escaping from an orange knitted bobble hat, she is a stark contrast to the other, mainly male walkers dressed in dark colours parking up to start their walks into the hills.

I hop into her van, because we've agreed she'll drive us both to the start of our adventure. In quiet tones over the noise of her VW engine, she explains we are going to the Nantlle Valley and from there we will walk for 40 minutes to below the mountain peak of

Craig Cwm Silyn. There are two lakes in its shadow, and we are going to swim in the one higher up.

Why that one? 'It is really clear and beautiful. It's like swimming in a glass of Evian. It doesn't really matter that it's a drizzly day like this because it is about the water. It is sublime. It is the most special just for the clarity of the water, and hopefully, especially on a day like today, there will be no one else up there.'

We wind our way up a narrow road. The purple heather and peaty soil surrounding us are spectacular. On our right a mountain ridge looms menacingly above us, and the sharp rocks look like a giant jagged shark's jaw. It is an eerie kind of day.

If our surroundings aren't spooky enough, she tells me that the name Nantlle can be translated to *screams* in Welsh. Legend has it that a monster used to live in the lake, and if anyone tried to swim across, he reached out with his long tentacles to drown them. Eventually, the villagers caught him, harnessed him and dragged him screaming all the way down the valley.

It turns out that her fear of what might be in the water is the reason we are here.

When Vivienne first moved to Snowdonia with her former husband nine years ago, she wasn't a swimmer but a rock climber. Together they used to spend days exploring the mountains, tackling increasingly harder routes. The more accomplished they became, the more she felt the urge to take time, stop and enjoy the view rather than rushing down after bagging yet another summit.

She was working as a teacher and using her degree in fine art to teach autistic children in a secondary school. She loved the teaching but hated being 'stuck inside a tiny box', as she puts it, from nine until three, and missed being able to express her own artistic imagination.

It sounds to me like she was looking for something to combine her creativity with her love of the outdoors.

Her life changed course when a friend who knew she enjoyed coasteering – clambering over rocks and jumping off them into the sea – introduced her to mountain swimming.

It wasn't love at first lake.

In fact, when she began, she was so scared of what might lie beneath that she would strap a camera to her chest and record every swim, to see what was there. Then she would race home to watch the recording – and catch only a fleeting glimpse of a tiny fish, or the flash of a fellow swimmer's hands or feet.

'The scariest thing in the lake is my ginormous magnified body. The fish are little tiddlers. There are no monsters.'

Vivienne started noticing the gracefulness of the swimmers, and the peace and serenity under the water, so she started taking pictures to try to capture it.

'I am an artist, and I really enjoyed sharing the images. I have really struggled with communicating verbally and in writing, but people liked it, it got noticed. People wanted to swim with me, and it became a business. I use the term *wild swimming* for my business, but I don't think there is anything remotely wild about it. For me wild swimming would be going down rapids in America. This is very gentle, serene.'

It doesn't feel like it is going to be very gentle or serene on a day like today.

Despite her fear that we might find nowhere to park, we are alone when we arrive at the car park, a small clearing marked out by rocks behind a rickety iron gate. One bedraggled sheep looks at us mournfully. When we get out of the van, the wind is howling. It is hard to hear each other as we set off, dressed head to toe in waterproofs, walking poles in our hands, heads down against the gale. The clouds are so low they surround us; it feels like we are being suffocated in their cold wet embrace.

We make our way gingerly over precarious stiles, following a lightly worn path through the heather, our boots sinking into murky puddles. She doesn't stop at the first lake, which looks bottomless and dark, a midnight black. It takes its colour from the soil and she assures me that the second lake is much more beautiful, surrounded by rocks which seep minerals into the water, making it clear and blue.

After 40 minutes trudging beside each other, I see the lake.

It is slammed up against the foot of a mountain and looks bleak and uninviting. The rocks encircling it, prehistoric and imposing, are jumbled on top of each other in perilous piles. Mist hangs over the water, the incessant wind is making it choppy and uneven. It looks steel grey not blue.

Despite the inclement conditions, there is no stopping Vivienne. We are already wet from the rain, so it doesn't matter that we get wetter as we undress for swimming. I am glad I brought my wetsuit because I am already cold. I am also relieved to know that she used to work as a lifeguard. Just in case of emergency, she is bringing a luminous buoyancy aid.

I think we must be bonkers. *Why on earth are we choosing to swim?* If Vivienne wasn't with me, there is no way that I would dream of venturing in, but she isn't hesitant.

'The entry is not attractive. It is really quite rocky and slippery, so take care. After that there is a beautiful reedy part, which we call the forest. You probably won't feel the reeds.'

I am not sure why, but after listening to her warning, I choose to go ahead of her. I put my bare toes in first, in the translucent water, and gasp. It is colder than I had imagined. That sharp, breathtaking cold which makes you struggle for air as your lungs contract.

Gingerly I submerse my, knees, my hands, shoulders, my face and – *Wow!*

What do I see?

Beautiful, calm, deep blue water all around.

The contrast between the wind and weather above the surface and the serenity underwater is overwhelming. I gasp, this time with surprise not cold. I have never seen our world so divided. Above the water, chaos. Beneath, tranquillity, an oasis. In that moment I understand why Vivienne does this.

'I like the nothingness, to see nothing but blue. Our lives are so busy. How often do you get that, no stimulation, nothing but you? It is my comfort zone, and I feel I can go in any weather because I am comfortable, and in any weather, you can always find a pocket that you can sink into.'

This is like nothing I have ever seen before.

Together we swim towards the far side, where the lake meets the mountain. We cross the still waters, a vast expanse of turquoise. I feel like I am swimming in space, weightless with nothing below me. Vivienne takes her time exploring underwater, inquisitive about what she can see. Together we swim over the rocks which have tumbled down the cliffs into the depths. They are stacked, higgledy-piggledy, an underwater avalanche. There is a strange shroud over them, a delicate, dusty veil. Magnificent but eerie.

I am unsettled as we make our way back to the shore, but am going to be brave and take off my wetsuit in the hope that Vivienne can take one of her magical pictures of me.

I strip down to my swimsuit, gasp again from the cold, and with my hands and feet totally numb try to obey her instructions.

Vivienne manipulates the huge and unwieldy camera, but it's hard work and she struggles in the water. At one point she tells me to take a deep breath and drop deep down. I do as she says, sinking hands above my head, like my version of a freediver. I surface a few seconds later and see relief written on her face. For a moment she had feared I wasn't going to come up again.

I can't swim for much longer because I can't move my hands; they are claw-like and numb. I take one last look over the reedy forest near the shoreline, spellbound by the pale green fronds reaching up to me as delicate and fragile as strands of hair.

I am exhilarated but frozen when we get out. My hands are white, and I can hardly move them. We both struggle to put on all our clothes, and as we leave the weak sunshine doesn't do much to warm us up. We stop to take pictures of a luminous rainbow stretching out beneath us in the valley, working out that her van must be right beside the pot of gold.

The cold has made me shaky and giggly as I listen to her tales of other swimmers who have shared the glorious beauty of the mountain lakes with her, including her last group who ended up going stark naked into the water.

'People are often very anxious, but the minute they get in the water it is joyous. It is so much fun, to see women able to be so happy and so free, and to be able to have the freedom to do that in the middle of nowhere and laugh like that is a joy.'

Huddled up and thawing out in the van, I ask her what her superpower is, and she says, *calmness*. I agree. Not only does she have an ability to be calm herself, but she passes that calm onto other people, a gift she makes more valuable by sharing. By daring us to peep below the surface, she shows us how to make our way through the chaos of life and find tranquillity.

Vivienne has shown me a world I had no idea existed. She has shaken my perspective and left me with a sense of beauty and serenity that I won't ever forget.

Weeks later, she sends me her photographs.

I love them.

They are ethereal and other-worldly. I am floating poised, calm and weightless, my limbs pale and luminescent against the blue-green stillness.

In my favourite, she has captured the moment when I scared her, when I took that deep breath and sank towards the bottom. You can see both the aubergine, amber hues of the mountain flank above the waterline, and the deep teal of the water below, a wave separating one reality from the other. It is like a painting of two realities.

I met Vivienne at an important junction in my life, just before leaving the job that began 20 years ago, presenting *BBC Breakfast*. I felt so fearful at the time. I knew I was taking a huge risk, but it was one that I felt I had to take. That photo perfectly encapsulates the feeling of relief as I took a deep breath and left a busy, stressful life getting up at 3.40 am, and relaxed into a calmer and more peaceful future.

# 11

# Kadeena Cox
## *Indoor Track Cycling*
## Lee Valley

Some people say you're faking it, there's nothing wrong with you, because they can't see it. And that's why I wanted to try to highlight invisible illnesses.

I am sitting on a wooden board, legs folded under me at the top of a wide ramp. One side of the ramp is covered in a pale blue carpet, the rest is bare concrete, painted a darker ocean blue. Directly in front of me is a black metal gate – open but uninviting because it leads to one of the scariest places I know. The entrance to a velodrome track.

This is not the first time I have been trackside, nor the first time I have braved the pine boards on two thin wheels, but the sight of the steeply sloped wooden sides still fills me with dread.

It seems fitting that I have parked myself on the ground to talk, because this feels like a safe and familiar space to be with my companion. I have spent countless hours with her chatting like this, lounging on filthy dirty flagstones in a dilapidated castle in North Wales when we were both contestants in *I'm a Celebrity . . . Get Me Out of Here!* (Sounds mad even to me, and I was there.)

I am with Kadeena Cox, one of the UK's most accomplished para athletes. She has six Paralympic medals to her name, including four golds, and currently holds two world records. Impressive enough, but when you consider she is the first British Paralympian for 32 years to win those medals in two different sports, athletics and cycling, you know she is a force to be reckoned with.

I knew it would be emotional to catch up with her today. I hadn't seen her since she left the castle a couple of nights before me, after an extraordinarily testing experience for both of us. We hug like sisters or long-lost friends, a hug that is tight, warm, life-enhancing.

I am here today because she has invited me to join her at a testing day for the KC (Kadeena Cox) Academy. She is dressed in a long-sleeved Rapha kit, which has been designed for her. It is an eye-catching orange, red, white and pink animal print that reminds me of a cheetah, and *KC Academy* is emblazoned across the chest.

It is wonderful to see her here. She looks relaxed, in control, and is positively glowing; this is her happy place. That's obvious from her body language and a smile dancing in her eyes.

This day is all about finding new cycling talent. She explains the reason she has set up an academy in her name is that she is the only Black British cyclist to win a gold medal at the Olympic or Paralympic Games. She wants to challenge the lack of diversity, particularly at the elite end of the sport – and today is part of her mission.

She is offering 16–30-year-olds the opportunity to try their hand at track cycling for free, to be put through their paces on and off the track. The offer was to cyclists of all levels – those who want to progress in this sport, and those who just want to give it a go.

The first thing we are taught is how to ride the bikes, which is very counter-intuitive. They have a fixed single gear and no brakes, and you can't freewheel. Stopping is even more confusing: you must keep your feet attached to the pedals, using your legs to slow the bike down, and must time this perfectly so that you can stop and put your hand on the safety rail near the exit.

Once we have learned this, we will do a timed 'flying lap' of 250 metres.

About 30 or so young people have turned up to take part, and I reckon that probably 70 per cent are men. It is Ramadan and seven of the candidates are fasting; they are told right from the start that there is no need for them to push themselves too hard, there will be another opportunity to put them through their paces.

It is immediately clear to me that we have very different levels of experience.

By the way some of them carry themselves, and how comfortable they are in the environment, I can see that there are some serious cyclists among us. Sure enough, a couple of them have brought along their very own snazzy, state-of-the-art carbon track bikes. There are others like me, who are essentially road cyclists and have been on a track maybe a couple of times. And then there are a handful of complete newbies, here for their first-ever taster session. What is lovely about the atmosphere today is that we are all made to feel equally welcome, and Kadeena is right at the heart of that.

'These days are really important, because I feel like there should never be a reason why someone shouldn't be allowed to do something – because of the colour of their skin, because of their religion, because of their orientation. You should never not be able to do something. I feel like cycling is a very white, middle-class sport. And there's no reason why we shouldn't be able to get people from other backgrounds in. I think there's potential for cyclists from Black backgrounds, for example, to be really strong, because you see it in athletics where they're really good. Why can that not be the same in cycling? I just think there's a lack of opportunity, the lack of support, the lack of feeling like they can do it, and the lack of role models.'

I remind Kadeena that she is the ultimate role model.

'There's me, but there's no one else. So, for men, you know, they've got no one to look up to. I'm trying to change that; the academy is about getting more people in at an elite level so there is that kind of representation. So, when you are looking up from the grassroots, young people can see people who look like them and think, *I look like them, maybe I can do it.*'

I have been in a velodrome twice before – and the first time changed my life. I was taking part in *BBC Breakfast*'s Presenters Christmas Challenge. We raced against each other in front of a crowd of 4000 people. The first time I went round the track I screamed, the second time I laughed, and the third time I loved it.

On the day of the race, I absolutely went for it and beat my co-presenter Bill Turnbull by a fraction of a second – meaning that my teammate Charlie Stayt and I won the *BBC Breakfast* gold. It was a terrifying, exhilarating experience and the moment I sprinted over the finishing line I had a lightning flash of revelation. In that half-second, I remembered that I *loved* competitive sport – and my life changed forever. I went on to represent my country in my age group in triathlon in World and European Championships, and it's the reason I'm writing this book, joining people like Kadeena on days like this, to tell her story.

Kadeena's introduction to track cycling also came about by chance and it too changed her life.

She was 23 and making a name for herself in track and field athletics, when she had a stroke. Subsequently she was diagnosed with multiple sclerosis. When her illness struck, she was in the process of changing sports from athletics to skeleton, but she wasn't allowed to continue. (In case you're wondering, skeleton involves a small sled and sliding down a frozen track face down and head first.) Even so, Kadeena was determined not to give up on a sporting career, and the person who had been overseeing her transfer between sports suggested that she should try either canoeing or track cycling instead.

'Because I couldn't run at the time, I'd been doing loads of stuff on the Wattbike [an indoor static bike], and it turns out I was relatively strong on it. So, I just jumped into track cycling, and loved it. I literally had never ridden the track until I had my stroke and I was diagnosed with MS. And it turns out, I'm pretty good at it. I don't think I ever would have tried it had I not got ill.'

I love Kadeena for her modesty. She is not just 'pretty good', she is currently the world record holder in her category (C4-5), setting the time when winning gold in the 500-metre time trial at the Tokyo 2020 Paralympic Games, held in 2021 (COVID again).

Her fortuitous encounter with cycling is another reason she wants other people like her to be given the chance. 'I think you should give people the opportunity to try out and see how good they are. Because, you know, until you try it, you never know.'

As we chat, she is at times distracted. Her gaze is on the track, and she is intently watching every single one of her potential academy members take their turn to set their fastest time. Each time the starting bell sounds for their wind-up lap, ahead of their 250 sprint, she shouts encouragement: 'UPPPPPP!'

I ask her what she is watching for, and she tells me she is intrigued to see what they can do, how they ride the track, how they use their power, how comfortable they are and whether or not they enjoy it. It is almost as if you can see people change before our eyes while we sit there.

One young man called Dele is very tall, has massive muscles and looks palpably strong. He tells me he is a rugby player, which makes sense as he is built like one. He would be terrifying on the pitch. The first thing he does when he is given his bike and sits on it, is to fall over onto his side. He has made the rookie mistake every cyclist makes: trying to put his foot down when his shoe is still attached to the cleat. He laughs as he lies on the floor with the bike still attached, on top of him. An hour later, on his flying lap, his raw power comes into its own: he flies round the track at breakneck speed, putting down a brilliantly fast time of 18.032 seconds. Less than a second behind the time set by Kadeena half an hour before.

I was on my bike on the track when she set that time and seeing her was astonishing.

I have watched her before, of course, but only from the comfort of my sofa. In the TV coverage she always looks strong, focussed and determined, in charge of not just the bike but also the track.

Here, now, as she comes past me, I can see her up close – and she is hypnotic. She seems to be part of the bike, melded to it, perfectly in tune with it, like liquid mercury moving around the track. And that's before she puts her foot down. When she does, it is like watching a thoroughbred racehorse released from the starting gate; you can see the surge of power and strength in her legs demanding the bike go faster. In less than 18 seconds she has covered the 250 metres, and as she zips past me over the finishing line, she dips her head out of habit, and as she continues slowing down, the smile across her face is infectious.

'I do love riding on the track. I love competing, and I haven't trained on the track in a while. So just being able to jump on my bike and do a flying effort – I was getting so excited, my legs were also dying, but that's not important. I loved it.'

Her sporting prowess is not the only thing I admire. Kadeena is very open about her eating disorder. 'Coming out of *I'm a Celebrity* and being deprived of food has made me be even more open about my eating disorder. I don't feel content with my body; since Tokyo I feel I have lost my sporting physique. Having an eating disorder and problems around food is very common in sport. The more I speak about that, the more people become comfortable with it and more people feel like they can reach out to have conversations. And you know, those conversations are a way of healing and a way of helping people to be able to get the support that they need.'

I loved my experience in *I'm a Celebrity*, and would do it all over again, but it was a tough environment. I was acutely aware that for someone with an eating disorder and multiple sclerosis it must have been even tougher.

Most of the time, Kadeena's MS was not obvious even to those of us in the castle, but there were a couple of occasions when things changed very suddenly and alarmingly. The first time, I noticed her speech change: she went from the bouncy, smiling, strong Kadeena to being unable to talk clearly. Her right arm and hand then went into spasms, and she lost control of her legs. She couldn't walk and needed someone to hold her up.

She has a fierce sense of pride and determination, and at the time I guessed that Kadeena would be reluctant to let people help.

'It was a very vulnerable moment but because I felt so comfortable with you guys I was happy to let you in; normally I would never let anyone help me in that situation. But I think because of the situation we were in and how close we became so quickly, I actually felt really happy with you helping me and comfortable enough to laugh my way through.'

And we did laugh. We laughed hysterically, especially when she put her arms over my shoulders and the shoulders of former

*EastEnder* Adam Woodyatt, and shouted out: 'Good leg, shit leg, good leg, shit leg' all the way to the loo and back.

For her, being seen on a massively popular television show was important. 'I think because a lot of people see me bouncing around riding my bike, you know, able to move around, they don't realise the struggles that I do have. And I think that's part of the reason why I wanted to do *I'm a Celebrity*, to show that behind the big, bold, smiley Kadeena there's a lot of struggles, a lot of pain, a real vulnerable side. And I think that's not just me, that's people with MS. Some people say you're faking it, there's nothing wrong with you, because they can't see it. And that's why I wanted to try to highlight invisible illnesses.'

I think it is a brave and powerful thing to do.

As I head home, I catch a glimpse of Kadeena on her knees on the floor beside one of the Wattbikes, helping one of the candidates attach the cleats on the bottom of their shoes to the bike pedals. She is concentrating hard, sharing her skills, passing on her passion – literally using her own hands to encourage the next generation. As I leave, I have no doubt that among the group today there will be more than one person whose cycling journey changes thanks to her.

The next time I see Kadeena we are both dressed up to the nines, with our make-up and hair done, ready to walk the red carpet at the National Television Awards. To our delight, our series of *I'm a Celebrity* wins an award. I have a drink (or two) to celebrate, but she stays off the alcohol. Wise move. Later that week she goes to the Para-cycling Track World Championships. It turns out to be the Great Britain cycling team's biggest medal haul to date, and Kadeena smashes her races. She wins two gold medals, one in the individual 500-metre Time Trial and the other in the Mixed Team Sprint.

That is not the last of her good news. Three of the first cohort of cyclists from the KC Academy have made the British

Cycling team and one of them, Sam Ruddock, is now a world champion.

When I ask her how she feels about that, she plays it down. 'It is pretty cool. I feel like I am making a difference in a small way.'

There is nothing small about what Kadeena has done. She is a fearless trailblazer. The choices she has made – to race, to set up her academy, to allow herself to be vulnerable on TV and show how MS affects her – are courageous decisions, which are changing perceptions and opening doors for others.

She knows that representation counts, that it can make a difference. She is the personification of *if you see it, you can be it.*

# 12

# Rhian Mannings
*Hiking*

## Snowdonia (Eryri)

> It is about living life to the full because we
> could so easily waste it and there is so much
> out there to explore.

The weather is gruesome.

I am engulfed by the cloud blanketing the top of the mountain. Rain is blasting into my face in freezing droplets. I am thankful for my woolly hat keeping my head warm, but my trousers are so wet that every time I bend my leg to climb another slippery step, I can see the water being squeezed out of them.

It is the middle of May, but it is only 2°C, and the gusts of wind whipping around me make it feel worse. I am cold, possibly dangerously cold, teetering towards hypothermia, but I don't want to admit it.

I huddle below the stack of rocks marking the summit and, with the help of my fellow walkers, I manage to pull on my waterproofs over my soaked trousers. I know my body temperature is plummeting, and I need to put on as many warm layers as I can, as quickly as I can. Shuddering and struggling with frozen hands,

I strip off my rain jacket and wriggle into a down one to wear underneath it. Luckily, I had packed it into a waterproof bag. I am frustrated that I followed the advice of one of our guides, who said that I didn't need to put on extra layers because this was just a passing shower. It wasn't. The weather has set in, and now I feel like an idiot; I should have listened to myself and trusted my instincts!

I am so intent on wrapping myself in layers that I nearly miss the celebratory photo starring those of us who have made it together up the Pyg Track to the summit of Snowdon (Yr Wyddfa). In it, you can just see me through the gloom, right at the back. The leader of our gang, Rhian Mannings, is right at the front with a huge smile on her face, unperturbed by the wild weather. She is holding a small white teddy bear in her left hand and hugging one of the other drenched hikers with her other arm. Rhian is a wonderful hugger and is ready to give one just when you need it.

The reason I am shivering at the top of the highest mountain in Wales is because I have joined a walk with a group of fundraisers. We are raising money for 2wish, a charity supporting those affected by the sudden death of a young person in Wales. It was set up in 2012 by Rhian in response to her own trauma.

This is just one of the three mountains that everyone else will attempt to climb in 24 hours. They are climbing the Welsh Three Peaks: Snowdon, Cadair Idris and Pen y Fan. I am waiting for a knee operation and know I can't make it to the top of all three summits but have decided I will at least try to get to the top of Snowdon and then decide. Right now, getting down this mountain safely seems like a challenge too far, let alone trying to climb another.

Our day had started in high spirits and bright warm sunshine. We met at what I think must be one of the world's most stunning car parks, at Pen-y-Pass, the highest point of the Llanberis Pass right in the heart of Snowdonia (Eryri in Welsh). It is nestled beneath green hills and rocky promontories. The ancient landscape, dominated by mountains sculpted by volcanos and glaciers, feels overwhelming.

Before we put even one foot on the path, I think that this is going to be my type of adventure: the first thing I see are copious snacks. Hot cups of tea, flapjacks, Scotch eggs and carefully buttered bara brith (Welsh tea bread) wrapped in baking paper. One of the volunteers has set up a table complete with white tablecloth, and it's laden with supplies.

Most of the group seem to know each other and chat happily while choosing their food. They have all been on the bus that left Llantrisant at 4 a.m. for the long drive up from South Wales. The hubbub is interrupted by our Expedition Leader for the day, Mark Lewis. He is ex forces and no-nonsense. As he gathers us round in front of him, he gets straight to the point about health and safety.

'As we go up, it is going to get colder, it is going to get windier, and potentially there could be some drizzle and rain. Where we are, it is about 13°. Up there, it is going to be about 5°. It is going to feel like it's freezing. The wind will rip through your trousers, which is why we recommend waterproof trousers, because they will act as a wind block. If you haven't got gloves, your hands will freeze, which makes your core get cold and that will affect your metabolism and your well-being. And if you start getting cold and your core gets cold, it starts to shut down – and your brain starts to shut down as well. There is a reason why we've asked you to bring the mandatory stuff – and to be sure you have, I want you to empty your bags in front of you and we will check it against our list. If you are missing something we will work around it, but you can't go up the mountain without it! OK?'

With that serious warning about the dangers ahead, all of us obediently turn our rucksacks upside down, spilling the contents onto the tarmac. Mark's safety team inspect the piles of belongings, making sure we have everything by ticking them off against a checklist.

It turns out I don't have enough water (2 litres), so I go and collect more from the car. Anyone who has crucial things missing, or who has left them on board the coach, is named and shamed and told firmly that they will be lent things here – but for the next mountain they must have all their own kit.

Rhian has everything, including a 2wish jacket, snood, woolly hat, hoody and T-shirt. She is also carrying a fluffy teddy bear, which she tucks inside the top of her rucksack, with its head poking out of the pocket. The bear is very special. It goes everywhere with her and has done so for the last 10 years. It is called Gorgeous George and is named after her baby boy who died after being taken ill very suddenly five days after his first birthday.

'It was his bedtime bear that he always slept with, and when he died, I wanted to keep it. I took it on my first adventure and now on any challenge he comes with me, peeking out the back of my backpack. I never wash him; I just dry him out when he gets wet. It is part of George coming with me everywhere I go. He goes on the front of my bike when I am cycling, and he's been on a walking marathon challenge. The only place he wasn't allowed to be with me was jumping out of a plane.'

Rhian's story darkened still further. Five days after the loss of baby George, her husband Paul took his own life. As we walk, she explains to me the horrific sequence of events.

'When you have young children, you have so much support from midwives and health visitors, and then when one of them dies, you hear from nobody. Everyone in the hospital was amazing and did everything they could for George, but when we left, we were given a piece of paper with some numbers on it, some of which didn't even work, and no other support.

'Left on our own, Paul and I blamed ourselves. You do with children, you know. If they fall over and break their arm, you feel guilty and responsible. And then when one of them is here one minute and in the next minute is gone, there was just nobody there to reassure us. I know that's why Paul took his own life, because he believed he was to blame, that he had failed our family, that he should have done more.

'We needed somebody with professional experience to explain to us that those feelings were quite normal after the sudden and dramatic death of a child. The reason I set up the charity is to stop people who have lost children suddenly and traumatically being left to go home and carry on their lives as normal, because that's not possible.'

Her double loss is unimaginable. Rhian was left to cope with the grief alone, and look after her other children, who were only two and three at the time.

I first met Rhian in 2017, five years after George and Paul had died, when I interviewed her on *BBC Breakfast*. She was taking part in *Mind Over Marathon*, a BBC One programme following 10 people affected by mental health issues, who trained for the London Marathon. I was struck by her calm grace in the face of adversity, and her story has stayed with me ever since.

As we head up the mountain, she tells me that she is still in contact with all of those who took part in the programme. That is the type of person Rhian is; she draws you in, puts her arms around you and makes you feel you want to be part of her family.

The first part of the Pyg Track is flattish but manageable and we make good progress as we talk, but after 20 minutes or so the big stone steps begin, and slow us down. I put my walking sticks in one hand and use my hands and knees to scramble up the rocks. It is a busy day in the hills and the track is narrow, so in some tricky parts we have to stop to make way for other hikers on their way down.

Rhian is chatting in front of me as we haul ourselves up and she tells me she had always intended to have more than three children. Being a mum was all she ever wanted to be.

I watch the gentle way she chivvies on the group and it strikes me that she is like a mother to all of us. Looking out for everyone, always watching, catching someone's eye and having a quiet word. 'Are you OK?' 'How is it going?' 'All good?'

She does this for me and for everyone else.

'It is so important to me; I just want everyone to be OK. I don't know if it is because of what happened to me, perhaps I felt I should have done more at the time when the boys died. I don't know, but I've always been a positive person who wants to look after everybody else, but since losing the boys I feel I want to make sure everyone is alright.'

She is a constant source of encouragement, even when the weather takes a turn for the worse.

We get the first inkling that there may be trouble ahead when we reach the saddle of the hill at Bwlch y Moch. It's a steep climb, and as we come over the pass, we can see the elevated path winding its way skyward towards the challenging Crib Goch scramble to our right. Down below us on our left we have a fabulous view of the dark waters of Llyn Llydaw. I know that standing there we should get our first glimpse of the summit of Snowdon, but today an inauspicious grey cloud hangs impossibly low, obscuring it from view. Still, at least the cloud will hide the perilous zigzags we will have to navigate to get to the top. Sometimes I find it easier psychologically not to be able to see what is ahead.

Given that our group has a range of different levels of fitness, we are sticking together well, but when our path joins the Miners'

Track and the rain sets in, it gets harder for our instructors to keep an eye on us. We keep being separated by other walkers making their way up or down.

As we stop for another break to let some of the stragglers catch up, I ask Rhian how she is doing.

'It has been tough, really tough. The weather isn't helping at all, but everyone is in good spirits; they are all egging each other on, and that is what it's about. It's character building.'

She is not wrong! I stand there shivering, waiting to go on up and feeling that my character is being built.

At the top it is clear the conditions are becoming treacherous; the temperature drops, and the stone path is wet and slippery.

Mark, who is in charge of safety, makes the call: our plan must change. The rain is turning to sleet and he concludes that it is too risky and dangerous for us to go back via the Pyg Track. It is even too cold for us to stop.

We will head down the much easier Llanberis Path. This is going to add about 2 kilometres to our walk, and about an hour to our journey, but it means we should all be safe.

I head down slowly, at the back of the group. Eventually, I catch up with Rhian, and we don't stop walking and chatting until we reach the Mountain Railway's Halfway station. I still feel frozen, and she gives me a huge hug to warm me up.

Before we reach the base of Snowdon and the entrance to the Mountain Railway, I can smell the unmistakable aroma of chips, and I share a cone of salty carbs laced with tomato ketchup and garlic mayo as the sunshine dries out my clothes. My mood lifts, and I decide that I will join them on their trek up the next mountain, Cadair Idris.

The delays caused by the dramatic weather mean we are late. We set off onto the Pony Path at 7 p.m., an hour and a half after we should have, and there is a collective groan when we are told that the trek will take us at least five hours. We will be lucky if we make it to the top before dark, and off the hill before midnight, so we are all armed with head torches and more warm clothes.

The walk is stunning. With the clouds gone we can see for miles – over forests, lakes and mountains. It is peaceful and quiet, and there is only our motley crew on the path, which meanders through an ancient woodland inhabited by gnarled, weather-beaten trees. A babbling brook keeps us company, as do tiny lambs flitting across the grass searching for their mothers. I watch their long tails wriggling in excitement as they suckle. The only interruption to our progress is metal kissing gates keeping the livestock safe.

Our first glimpse of the sinking sun, reflecting off the sea miles below us, gives us a lift and a real sense of achievement. Despite our fears we are making great progress, and though I am not sure how far the summit is, right now I don't care; I am enjoying the journey.

As nightfall starts to envelop us, we gingerly pick our way over scree and sharp, ankle-breaking rocks, and then the path gets steeper. When we pause for a breather, I notice that occasionally Rhian steps aside, removes herself from the group, lost in thought.

'I sometimes stop and think, *What am I doing?* Before, I had never done anything like this. When I am walking, I think about the boys and what they would say and what they would think of it. I can't help it. I think about them all the time. I do a lot of these things because I think Paul and George will never be able to breathe our air again and hear the birds singing and see the sun rise. And I sometimes feel like I want to live a life for them as much as myself. It is about living life to the full because we could so easily waste it and there is so much out there to explore.'

If Paul knew what she was doing, what would he make of it?

'He wouldn't be surprised to see me trying to be positive. I used to always be the arranger and organiser. But now he wouldn't recognise the things I do, the running, the cycling. Everything is new since I lost him. All of this is new to me, and I just hope that he is proud of me, and that George would be proud of me as well.'

We head back to the path, which is getting more challenging. Right at the end, at the top of the ridge, there is a last scramble. Pulling ourselves over boulders in the gathering darkness is deeply challenging but worth every second of effort and each of us reaches up to touch the top of the trig point. This time I am not cold, wet or worried, and my smile is as wide as Rhian's as we stand at the top taking a selfie with George the bear.

I love Snowdon, but there is something especially magical about Cadair Idris, enhanced by the time of day. The light has gone completely as we head towards home, and each of us switches on our head torch so we can find our footing. Seeing the sprinkle of lights bobbing ahead, I think it looks like a pilgrimage from a bygone era. Rhian agrees it looks romantic as I fall into step with her and her best friend, Andrea.

The two of them first met on the night George was admitted to hospital. Andrea was one of the nurses who tried to save his life.

'When George died, Andrea really looked after us, and did all she could under extreme pressure. Wales is a very small place, and a while later I was out somewhere and I recognised her. I ran off but my sister spoke to her and realised she lived a couple of miles from where I live. After that we met for coffee, and we started meeting a little bit and she massively helped me. I think seeing me helped her because she really struggled with her role after finding out that Paul had died. Now we are best friends.'

I notice Andrea is hobbling. She has a sore knee but is determined to keep Rhian company; they go everywhere together and are virtually inseparable. Rhian has that impact on people: she inspires loyalty and affection. There is something about her that draws you in.

I think we must be nearly back at base when a shout goes up from behind us: we have gone the wrong way! We took a left too soon.

We retrace our steps, and when we finally reach the car park it is six minutes past midnight. Rhian gives me another of her restorative hugs and I wish them good luck on their onward journey. All of us are tired and sore and I don't envy them as they head south in the coach; they have only a couple of hours before it's time to tackle Pen y Fan.

Despite sore joints, exhaustion and an injury, they all managed it. At the summit of the third peak, they lit tea lights in memory of the 1100 children and young adults who have died suddenly, and whose families and friends have been supported by the charity.

It is important work, and Rhian knows from the emails she receives that the charity saves lives. She has had many messages from fathers urging her not to judge Paul or to be angry with him. They tell her it was the support of 2wish that helped them make a different choice for themselves.

'I can never bring back Paul and George, however much I'd like to, but what I can hopefully do, through their legacy, is make sure that other people feel that they are not alone. We can't take away their pain, we can't bring back their children, but what we can do is make sure that if they need us that we are there.'

A couple of days after our epic walk, I catch up with Rhian. She is tired but already looking forward to her next challenge, climbing Kilimanjaro.

I ask if George the bear is going, and she laughs and says yes – although she is thinking of getting him a raincoat to keep him dry.

# 13

# **Mimi Anderson**
## *1200km Cycle Across Argentina*

I do full-on crying as I'm running along. I cry because that is how my emotions come out. And how I tend to get rid of stress. I cry and then I'm alright.

I am in my own version of hell.

My feet are swollen, burning in my cycling shoes that are claustrophobically tight. Relentless, blistering heat is scorching the tarmac. It rises in waves, envelops me, surges through the underside of my bicycle seat, drags me down. The air feels thick and heavy, my chest is constricted. I feel as if I am suffocating, unable to breathe and panicky.

The heat has stolen what was left of my depleted reserves of courage. I have nothing left. I have been fighting a feeling of dread, trying desperately to ignore it, but when I think of what my husband David would say if he could see me now, it becomes too much. I have to give in and ask my cycling companion to stop. I am too scared to go on.

I am about 350 kilometres and three days into a 1200-kilometre cycle ride from the border of Chile high in the Andes across the vast pampas of Argentina to Buenos Aires. I have been on my bike pedalling as hard as I can since dawn. When I left the hotel, the moon was still hanging low in the inky blue sky, like a parchment puppet held by invisible string. Now it's past midday and the sun is beating down. The heat is shimmering off the road. I feel like I am hallucinating: the road is so straight that it seems to rise vertically into the sky. I feel discombobulated; my brain tells me it is physically impossible for the road to be rising, but my eyes are telling me different.

I call out to my travelling companion, who has been ahead of me for the last hour, unwavering in her pace, empowered by the sunshine, cycling fluidly, like a well-oiled machine. She embodies fierce determination and strength, the exact opposite of how I feel.

'Mimi, can I stop?'

'Sure, what's up?'

'I am scared. I need to stop!'

Without any hesitation, she pulls off the road, onto the gravel of the hard shoulder.

I follow. My shoulders relax with relief, and I unclip my shoes from my pedals and step down into a wide dry ditch beside the road, as far as I can be away from the traffic and in what I hope is a safe place. I park my bike on the parched earth under a spindly tree with sharp spikes on it. In its paltry shade, I try to get my breath and courage back.

It is 38°C and we have been battling into a strong headwind along the RN7, a dual carriageway that is the main artery joining Chile and Argentina. It is not very busy, because right now the border between the two countries is closed, but travelling on my bike is terrifying. Dozens of HGVs have thundered past me at frightening speed, and I have been quivering with terror, trying to make myself both visible but small, trying both to make sure they see me and to get out of their way, my hands shaking on the handlebars.

The reason I am so scared is that we no longer have our safety vehicle with us. It had been driving right behind us, mile after relentless mile, and protecting us from the worst of the lorries, its flashing hazard lights slowing them down.

Without the protective barrier of the minibus behind us, my newsreader mind has been going to dark places, reminding me in a loop of all the bad news stories of accidents involving cyclists.

That's how I've ended up in the baking heat on the side of the road with one of the most accomplished endurance athletes in the world – who, as it turns out, has the patience of a saint. She is smaller than me, wiry and fierce in a way that I wish I was. (Plus she has an impressive shock of thick white hair, which always looks as if she has just stepped out of the hairdresser, rather than being halfway through an epically tough bike ride across Argentina.)

Mimi Anderson is a 60-year-old grandmother of four – and in the world of endurance running, a legend. She has smashed world records across the globe. She has won extreme races in deserts in blazing heat, in the frozen Arctic, and in the humidity of the Peruvian jungle, and she is a multiple Guinness World Record holder.

It is difficult to get my head round her extraordinary achievements, and also to understand why she isn't a household name. My hunch is that, if she had been a man, we would know all about her running records – and I would have interviewed her on the *BBC Breakfast* sofa.

Let me list just a few of her achievements.

In 2007 she won the 6633 Arctic Ultra, an extreme marathon in the Arctic, covering 352 miles in 143 hours, 23 minutes, and enduring temperatures as low as -70°C. She is still the record holder, because the course itself has now changed.

In 2008 she became the female world record holder for running from John o' Groats to Land's End. It's a journey of 1352 kilometres, which took her 12 days, 15 hours and 46 minutes. (Her record was beaten only in 2020 by Carla Molinaro.)

In 2014 she was the only finisher in the Cyprus Ultra, setting a new course record.

She also holds the World Record for running the length of Ireland: 555 kilometres from Malin Head to Mizen Head in three days, 15 hours and 36 minutes.

Not only has she completed and won dozens of the world's toughest races, but very often she has done the double – running from the start to the finish and back again, or the other way round, just for fun.

Despite her long list of incredible running titles, Mimi wasn't born a runner. She struggled with anorexia for many years and first tried running at the age of 36 because she had issues with her body image. Specifically, she didn't like the look of her legs; she wanted them to be slimmer. Her first run was on a treadmill in her local gym, where she couldn't run for more than 30 seconds without getting out of breath. When she managed her first mile, she cheered with joy.

After that, she graduated to running outside with friends, and within a couple of months, they had signed up for one of the most gruelling races on the planet, the terrifying Marathon des Sables. This is a multistage event that takes place over six days in Morocco in the inhospitable Sahara Desert. Competitors run 250 kilometres over sand dunes and salt lakes, carrying all their provisions on their back. Her first endurance race was excruciatingly tough, and she very nearly had to pull out because of a stomach bug, but she refused. When she was at rock bottom, she was galvanised to carry on by the words of a friend who took her to one side and said:

'Imagine all of those people who think you can't do this!'

That was the motivation she needed to finish – and when she did, she was hooked. She went on to become a serious athlete, revered in the running community. As I have my crisis of confidence on the side of a South American highway, I am in illustrious company.

I had met Mimi only a week before at Heathrow airport in a desolate Terminal 5, deserted because it was 10 p.m. on a Saturday night and travel was still being affected by the pandemic. We met ahead of a long flight to Santiago, on our way to be 'test pilots' for a race across South America. The ride was meant to be from Valparaíso on Chile's Pacific coast to Buenos Aires on the Atlantic coast, but COVID had closed the border between the two countries. Mimi, other cyclists and myself made it to the starting point, but our Expedition Leader didn't manage it, nor our Safety Crew. That forced a quick change of plan, and we are now cycling across Argentina from its western mountain border to the eastern seaboard, a journey of about 1287 kilometres.

By the roadside, in the blazing sunshine, Mimi stands by her bike, cool as a cucumber, not wilting like me under the scarce shade of the tree. She could not be more understanding and sympathetic about my overactive imagination. I watch as she mainlines Haribos and scans the horizon for our van. This is about teamwork, she reassures me, and calms me down by saying: 'You have to follow your instincts, and your instincts are telling you that it isn't safe, and you need to stop – and that is fine with me. We will wait.'

Wait we did.

To me the minutes seemed interminable, but she never hinted at leaving me, and when the van eventually caught up with us, I had calmed down and we got back on our bikes, battling onwards in the baking heat. I felt completely better only when, after another 30 kilometres struggling to stay safe on the dual carriageway, we made our way to a smaller road and found a café in a tin shack selling Coca Cola. I recovered by making my way through most of a kilo pack of deliciously salty crisps.

In contrast to the baking heat on the dual carriageway, our journey had started in freezing cold temperatures at the dizzying height of 3832 metres under the imposing statue of Cristo Redentor de los Andes – Christ the Redeemer of the Andes. The impressive symbol of peace overlooks the highest point of the old road at La Cumbre between Santiago, the Chilean capital, and Mendoza in Argentina's wine country.

The 7-metre high bronze sculpture of Christ couldn't be a more dramatic location for the start of a journey. It is surrounded by snow-capped peaks, azure blue skies, and tantalising glimpses of South America's highest mountain, the sleeping giant that is Aconcagua.

The first part of our descent is heart-stoppingly perilous. A steep dirt track, which takes you round a series of spectacular but scary hairpin bends and switchbacks. The surface is a nightmare to navigate – sometimes deep sand, sometimes gravel, sometimes bone-jarring ruts. In addition, a steady flow of taxis and tourist minibuses slip and slide, struggling to get traction while trying to overtake. I have to stop every few minutes to stretch my hands and wrists, which are cramping from trying to feather the brakes. And I'm doing my best to ignore the dramatic drops over the side. But the view and kaleidoscope of colours make up for the pain: a stunning palette of coppers, rusts, browns and beiges fade into the sunlight behind the mountain peaks.

Mimi is more nervous than I am and missed out the gravel part of our descent, travelling downhill in the back of the support vehicle. When we hit the smooth tarmac on our way down towards Uspallata, and the road snakes endlessly in front of us through a deep valley, she is behind me. I go as fast as I dare, enjoying the speed, and then wait for her to catch up. Invariably, as soon as we hit any sort of an incline, she pulls ahead. She is much stronger cycling uphill and I am more courageous going down. I get braver as the miles roll beneath our wheels and when I let myself fly down one steep hill, my whoops resonate round the valley. Later I see that I hit 67 km/h on my speedometer.

The vistas are vast and breathtaking. We fly alongside a wide, dry riverbed, sheer cliffs framing the banks, interrupted by rock formations so architectural in structure they look like gothic cathedrals built out of purple and blue stone. It is ancient landscape, reminiscent of an untouched Martian desert. I feel tiny, insignificant.

Mimi says it reminds her of an ultramarathon called Badwater in Death Valley, which runs through an area called Artist's Drive. I love Mimi because she has a story for everything.

That first day, safely in the hotel as we lay on our beds chatting after dinner, Mimi says she can't understand how people cycle so fast. 'I think I am doing really well, and people just go vroom past me. I think, *How have they done that? Perhaps I'm in the wrong gear?* I go up a gear, then I can't pedal, so I go down again, and it's not enough, so I must be in the wrong gear, and that's why I haven't got the oomph. All these things are going through my head and I have to remember that they will come. I have to remember when I first started cycling, I couldn't even take my left hand off the handlebars. I couldn't do that. And I wasn't clipped in. All these things and I couldn't do them, but they will come.'

By 8 a.m. on Day 2, our camp is a hive of activity as everyone gets their bikes ready. Mimi is a vision of brightness. She's wearing a turquoise and pink cycling jersey with flamingos on it, a pink cycling helmet, pink arm warmers, pink snood and pink socks. The only thing that isn't pink is the gravel bike she calls Pebbles, which is a metallic dark orange, the colour of Berocca. I have matched my outfit to hers as much as I can – pink and turquoise but not quite as bright as hers.

We have already settled into a wonderful rhythm both on and off the bike. On the bike she is in charge of navigation, and I am in charge of snacks.

On Day 2 the ride from Uspallata in the foothills of the Andes and onto Rivadavia is sensational. I am transfixed by the impeccably groomed and regimented lines of vines in the lush green vineyards outside Mendoza, and think wistfully about stopping for a glass of Malbec.

Much of today's ride is downhill, but the hills there are, are long and arduous. I am struggling to keep my heart rate down and find myself short of breath and trailing behind Mimi, who is strong and steady as an ox.

Just when I'm beginning to think I couldn't manage another incline, we turn a corner to be greeted by the sight of the aquamarine water of Potrerillos Reservoir stretching out beneath us. We stop to take a photo of the glacial blue water wrapped around tiny rocky islands. The others are probably miles ahead of us, but we agree we want to take this in.

That night as I hang my bike from the branch of a lime tree and clean it, Mimi discovers why she is going slower than she hoped. She has been complaining that her bike is squeaking, as if there is a mouse on board. One of the team has a closer look and notices both of her brakes are permanently on. No wonder she has been struggling!

As I watch them laughing and drinking beer as they fix it, I realise I am in one of my happy places, where I have already had a life-changing adventure.

I spent a year living in Argentina when I was 21 years old, and I was in my third year at university, studying Spanish. It feels life-affirming to be back after 30 years.

When I arrived, I spoke very little Spanish. My lack of application, coupled with the complications of the Argentinian accent, meant I hardly understood anything. On my first day at work in a cotton thread factory on the outskirts of Buenos Aires, I was asked what language I wanted to speak. In the half second before replying, I thought: *Well, I haven't travelled 7000 miles from home not to learn the language,* so I took a deep breath and said: 'Spanish!'

From that moment on I was catapulted into a crash course in communication. It was total immersion; I could do nothing if I didn't understand what people were saying. I had to learn – and learn fast. Four months later, I was in love with the language, in love with the literature, and dreaming in Spanish.

When I returned to university virtually bilingual, my professors were staggered by the change in me.

Now I am back after three decades away, and words, songs and memories that have formed part of my character but which have been hiding from view now have the space to reappear, and they make me smile.

Of course, my Spanish also means I am very useful for ordering food in restaurants, always asking for more salt and extra chips!

The blistering heat of our third day, when I had to stop on the dual carriageway, is broken by a monumental thunderstorm that shakes us awake in the middle of that night. The rain hammering on the corrugated iron above our heads sounds biblical and I am worried we are going to be blown away.

The next morning, we have to set off a little late because the roads are flooded by the sheer volume of rain – and when we do, all eight of us cycle together in a tight and fast peloton. Mimi and I manage, just, to keep up until our first stop at 30 kilometres when she says she needs to slow down. The peloton speed is making her nervous, and she can't eat or drink on the bike, and she needs the calories to keep her fuelled.

After that we are back in our happy pair and cycling in tandem down long avenues, with tall trees leaning over us. Every few metres parakeets shout out a warning to each other as we pass, chirping in alarm. The area feels much more agricultural, and far less monied. There is hardly any traffic on the potholed rural roads and any cars or trucks we see are impossibly old and dilapidated. They trundle past us at slow speeds, listing to one side, and seem to be held together by not much more than hope and string.

We are heading towards the metropolis of San Luis. It is much bigger than I remember. I recall wide, empty streets with tumbleweed floating down the dirt roads. Now I see a huge, bustling city, its skyline dominated by dramatic modern architecture.

I have been worried about the hills beyond San Luis, knowing that I am the weakest of the two of us when it comes to any kind of gradient. Faced with an ascent, Mimi switches into endurance mode, head down, cadence low. She slowly pulls ahead of me, and I can only hope that I can get to the top in time for me to catch her on the way down.

We are having a great day, making good time and stopping for a picture – and we don't look behind us to see heavy clouds moving fast towards us, about to dump their cargo right on top of us.

The rain, when it comes, is fierce and furious. There is no shelter in sight, and the tarmac is now slick with puddles bouncing from the deluge. We have no choice but to hunch up our shoulders, scrunch up our eyes, and ride through the storm, trying to ignore the raindrops as sharp as electric shocks, like needles pricking our bare skin. It hurts, but we carry on.

We eventually find respite in our minibus, which is parked for safety under a road bridge, and leave our bikes perched against the walls. We're just in time: as soon as we shut the door of the bus behind us, the storm dials up another notch. Lightning flashes on the fields in front of us, and the thunder rolling round above us makes us shudder. There is so much water streaming down the banks it forms rivulets and soon I can't see the road.

We eat and try to keep warm. The heat from our bodies steams up the windows. I am delighted to be inside, and secretly hoping that might be it for the day, that we will have to stop and be driven the rest of the way because carrying on is too dangerous.

Mimi almost speaks my exact thoughts. 'Part of you in your head is thinking, *Wouldn't it be nice if the storm stayed all day? And then we wouldn't have to get out of the coach and cycle all the way to our hotel because it'd be too dangerous.* Sometimes on a long ultrarun I will think, *If I twist my ankle here, and fall down a hole, I won't have to go on.*'

I look at her with my eyes wide. I thought it was just me who had those type of negative, defeatist thoughts.

'And then another part of you is thinking, if you did that you would be pathetic, you would feel you had let yourself down. Because you haven't got on your bike, and you haven't cycled. So, I will carry on, but only if they let us go!'

She talks about the many races when she has felt like this, and the many moments of doubt, and I ask her how she gets through them.

'I break it down into manageable chunks. I don't bother looking at how fast I'm going because I just can't, I physically can't go any faster, so it is irrelevant, really, isn't it? The chunks could be a distance, it could be something you're heading towards like an object, something you can see up ahead, a tree, a signpost. And then when you get really knackered you literally run from lamp post to lamp post.'

We have all settled in, enjoying Mimi's storytelling, and there is a perceptible groan after 40 minutes or so when the bus door is opened by Phil Briggs, our Race Director, who tells us that we need to get back on our bikes.

We do so reluctantly, and much to our dismay slam into a fierce, relentless headwind. It feels like we are going backwards; we are both really struggling. One of the things that has been keeping me going is the signposts telling me how many miles we are from Buenos Aires. The road here is so small they are gone now, and not having them to count me down makes it feel worse.

We must have looked desperate because Katherine Bond, one of our fellow riders, who has been taking a rest in the van, gets out to give us a hand. Courageously she rides in front and protects us from the worst of the buffeting. Together we battle onwards until the wind changes to a crosswind, and we gather speed as she teaches us to echelon. Positioning our bikes at angles to each other, we are protected from the wind and gather speed. Not only does this save our energy, but we start eating up the miles.

Mimi is over the moon: in one day she has gone from being nervous riding in a peloton to managing to handle a very technical cycling manoeuvre. We are loving it!

The next morning our short-lived euphoria evaporates. Our journey has come to a sudden halt. One of the riders in our peloton and our minibus driver have tested positive for COVID. For safety reasons we can go nowhere until we have a new driver, and everyone else tests negative.

Mimi and I are chatting, lying side by side on a thin mattress on a double bed in a hotel – a hotel that has gone straight into my Top 10 of the worst I have ever stayed in.

Mimi is not afraid of hardship, though; she just doesn't care, in a way that I wish I could adopt. She has raced in all conditions: the searing heat of the Kalahari Desert, the freezing cold of the Arctic, and the energy-sapping humidity of the Peruvian jungle. All were multi-day events with no respite; relentless and with no chance of a shower or a long night's sleep in a clean bed.

Often, she has raced entirely self-sufficiently, having to carry everything she needs in a tiny backpack: medical supplies, sleeping bag, hammock, food and water. I ask her how she copes.

'It's what you sign up for, isn't it? I know when I sign up for an event, it is going to be tough. I try not to think about it too hard, because I probably wouldn't sign up. I think: *I am signing up because it is a place I want to go and see*, so whether that's the Arctic or the jungle, the camping and the hardship and everything that goes with it is part and parcel of that journey to that location. It is part of what makes it special.'

Her attitude is no-nonsense. You signed up, so suck it up and get on with it! When that doesn't work, she resorts to a couple of things: tears and laughter.

She tells me about the time in South Africa when she was doing the double at the Comrades Marathon. It is one of the world's hardest races, a 90-kilometre ultramarathon characterised by endless tough hills. Mimi being Mimi, she chose to do it twice in one go. Comrades has an 'up' year (Durban to Pietermarizburg) and a 'down' year (vice versa). On the down year, she began her double in Durban, ran to the finish in Pietermarizburg, before going back to the official start where she joined all the other runners racing back to Durban. She finished and became the first woman to do so, but she had difficult moments on the way.

'On that race I had a mini meltdown. On one of the aid stations my bottle wasn't where I thought it was going to be. When you are tired, something as stupid as a bottle not being in the right place really annoys you and I cried. I do full-on crying as I'm running along. I cry because that is how my emotions come out. And how I tend to get rid of stress. I cry and then I'm alright. It doesn't happen very often. I mean, on a big race it can happen probably a couple of times.'

I know exactly what she means about the power of a good cry.

I love how Mimi uses laughter to deal with hardship too. She tells me about the time she was struggling while trying to hang up her hammock for the night in the jungle during a five-day stage race in Peru. The only time she had done this previously was in her garden in Kent.

'I remember on that race, when we set up our first hammocks in the jungle in these hammock stations, we had these macaws screeching around us and we were struggling, exhausted and desperate for rest. Finally, we got them up and we all tried to get into them, and everything collapsed. It was very funny. It was like a concertina. You're knackered and you're at altitude, you haven't got a bed, but you have to laugh.'

I ask her about her toughest challenge ever, without which we wouldn't be on a cycling adventure together. To talk about it makes her indomitable voice falter and brings tears to her eyes.

In 2017 Mimi was 40 days and 3565 kilometres into a world record attempt to run across America when a knee injury literally stopped her in her tracks. After averaging almost 92 kilometres a day, she had developed a lean to the left so bad that if she didn't concentrate, she felt as if she was going to fall over. Waking up on Day 41, she was in so much pain she could hardly walk. That day her support group had to meet her every mile, and every time she saw them, she burst into tears. At mile 16, it was too much. She stopped and they booked in for an MRI scan. The news wasn't good: no cartilage on the outside of her right knee, and swelling of the bones both below and above the knee, which could cause multiple stress fractures if she continued. The consultant warned her there was a chance she could end up going home in a wheelchair.

The light fell out of her world, and five years later what happened still brings her grief and pain. I feel guilty that I have asked her about it, as I watch her trying to hold back tears.

'I felt very ashamed, a failure, because I hadn't got to New York. I hid in New York for a week or so. I just couldn't bear going home and seeing anybody. It was awful. It was the worst feeling. Most times when you have a failure, there is always a way to turn it around into a positive, you can always learn from it. A failure is never a failure if you can learn something from it. I have tried and tried and tried to find something positive about that. And I couldn't think of anything. I still struggle with it now. I covered a massive distance; I did an incredible thing. I had the courage to stop – for me that's a really big thing – but I can never go back and do it again. Usually if you have a failure, you go back and try again, but with this one I can't do that event again.'

That is where Mimi is different from many of us. She is fearless, determined to just keep trying. If she fails, she will try and try again. Not everyone does. Many of us give up in the face of failure, turn away or stop trying, because we are too scared or humiliated to fail again. Mimi is different: apart from America, which she can't physically repeat because of the severity of her injury, she has always gone back to finish what she started.

After her disappointment, and facing the prospect of never being able to run long distances again, Mimi talked to a fellow runner who had suffered a similar injury. He advised her to accept as quickly as possible that she would never be able to run and suggested she tried cycling – which is why we are here!

She bought her first bike that January and the following September completed Ride Across Britain, a 9-day event over 1560 kilometres. She didn't feel like a natural cyclist, and says she looked like a runner on a bike sitting up far too straight. She had to learn how to use drop handlebars, and she fell off five times while trying to use clipped-in pedals. Despite that, she did it, and, as she says, *almost* loved it!

Since then, Mimi has cycled thousands of miles, including the Pacific Coast Highway from Vancouver to California's Imperial

Beach. Even so, when I am with her, she calls herself a *bike-list* not a cyclist. That is one of the most noticeable and refreshing things about Mimi: she wears her considerable success lightly. She is one of the most accomplished but modest people I have ever met.

After 24 hours out of the saddle, our COVID interlude over, we are relieved and excited when we are allowed back on our bikes again.

We do the first 60 kilometres in record time and Mimi is chuffed because our average speed is a very respectable 28 km/h, not bad for *bike-lists*. As ever, I am looking forward to the pit stops.

They happen every 30 kilometres, unless we happen to be on a very dangerous bit of road where stopping would compromise our safety. Given we are covering a daily average of about 170 kilometres, we have about five stops a day.

There is a reassuring routine. Our support team scoot ahead of us, tooting and waving cheerily as they go past and set about finding a suitable spot far ahead of us to set up camp on the side of the road. It might be under the shade of a tree, or beside a vineyard, or perhaps with a view of a river. Every stop is different. Some picturesque and some less so, but they always make an effort.

When they stop, they fire up a mini stove by the side of the truck to heat up water so the coffee lovers among us can have a dose of caffeine, and then open the back of the truck and lay their wares out, like a food stall at a festival. The menu changes from day to day, depending on where we are and what they can find.

Snacking is one of the reasons I love cycling, but Mimi finds it more difficult than me and has to make an effort to eat enough to keep going. She fills herself with ham sandwiches and occasional crisps and biscuits.

As I sit with my snacks, slowly rejuvenating, I watch Mimi. She is always laughing raucously, holding her water bottle aloft as if drinking a glass of wine in a packed pub, and being waited on hand and foot. This self-confessed cycling newbie has been adopted by the team, taken under their wing, and is adored by everyone. She is the life and soul of the party, entertaining everyone with epic stories of high jinks and adventures.

She is upbeat and optimistic, the positive teammate making sure that everyone is OK and morale is kept high. Her joie de vivre is contagious.

We are now a week into our ride, and having spent almost every minute of every day within two metres of each other, Mimi and I are finely tuned to each other's moods and movement.

My usual position is to ride just behind Mimi. I watch her back, subconsciously noting the distinctive bobbing of her head, making sure the cadence of my pedalling matches hers. I can see that she is working hard, her legs pumping *one two*, *one two*, as steady as a metronome, determined to mark down the miles.

We are cracking on at a respectable 27 km/h when suddenly I notice that something is wrong. Her speed drops very suddenly – and with no warning she pulls off the road onto the gravel. She says she doesn't feel good, but she doesn't need to tell me, I can read it in her face. She is pale and sweaty, sweatier than I have seen her. The heat is her friend, she thrives in it, is powered by it, so that's not the problem. When I feel as bad as she looks, I need food – and I need it quickly. I delve into my emergency food bag and grab some glucose tablets and sweet jelly shots. She snaffles them all.

Mimi is human after all! She has bonked, as they call it in cycling. Bonking is no fun. She has literally run out of fuel, and like a car with no petrol has come stuttering to a stop by the side of the road.

She didn't eat well last night, and has been chasing nutrition all day, drinking Coke at all our pit stops and seemingly unable to quench her thirst. Finally, the effect of not having enough calories has stopped her.

The effect of the sugar on her bloodstream is incredible. Within the space of only five minutes the colour comes back into her cheeks, the sparkle is back in her eyes, and she is ready to get back on her bike to finish off the day.

Our last day is a testing one.

We have 187 kilometres to get from Arrecifes to Buenos Aires. We are told that if we don't make good time, we will have to put our bikes in the minibus and be driven. Mimi and I are having none of that, so we set off with gusto. It's an emotional day right from the start and a tough one because the roads into the city are fast and dangerous. We are told we must stick together to stay safe, but we get separated from the rest of the group on a dual carriageway, which scares me. We are still on our own, riding through the bustling side streets of the barrios and trying to avoid buses with black clouds of smoke coming from their exhausts, when another cyclist passes and warns us: 'Don't slow down here – they will steal your bike from you.'

That makes me more anxious – for all of us – and when we finally catch up with our group, I cry with relief.

The final few miles are great fun. All of us are together, keeping a close eye out for potholes, slowing for traffic lights, calling out to each other to warn of obstacles, swooping over roundabouts in unison. I shriek as I stutter over cobbles in San Fernando, my bike juddering in complaint, and breathe a sigh of relief as we finally draw alongside the mighty Río de la Plata lazily flowing towards the sea. We are nearly there now.

The end, when it comes, is disappointing. The sky is heavy and loaded with dark, menacing clouds. The sea is grey and choppy, cold and uninviting. There is no beach to speak of, and the vegetation is too thick for us to dip our toe in the South Atlantic.

Nothing, though, will diminish our sense of pride and camaraderie. Together we all lift our bikes above our heads and cheer in triumph.

I have enjoyed every minute of being with Mimi. She was one of the first women who inspired me to write this book and I feel very lucky that she has let me join her on this adventure.

I ask Mimi how she feels. 'I think my body is extraordinary. I went through many, many years where I hated my body. It didn't matter how thin I got; it was never right. All I could see was this fat person looking back at me. I could never see what other people saw. But my body has done extraordinary things. It's enabled me to run around the world and it has enabled me to do what we've done in the last few days. I've had children; that alone is a special thing. So I now look at my body in a completely different way. I don't want those thin, skinny legs that I wanted before. Now they are strong, and they've enabled me to do incredible things – and that is what it is all about.'

I can entirely relate to how she feels about her body. I think many of us women are damagingly negative about our body shape, constantly comparing ourselves to others, wanting to change, and forgetting what incredible things our bodies are capable of. Concerns about body image burn through so many of these chapters.

Mimi reminds us to celebrate our bodies not for what they look like but for what they enable us to do.

# 14

# Lizzie Carr
## *Standup Paddleboarding*
### River Trent, Nottinghamshire

> When you're faced with death, the reasons you want to live suddenly become over-whelmingly clear – and that is what you fight for.

I reach out a cold hand and grasp the tip of what looks like a brand-new red traffic cone, which is sticking up like a warning beacon out of the silty brown water. It is stuck to the bottom, and moves with a satisfying squelch only when I give it a double-handed heave, which very nearly pitches me headfirst off the side of my paddleboard into the river. I haul it dripping with slimy sludge onto the pristine surface under my knees, and smile. I never knew that picking up rubbish could feel so good. That feeling of satisfaction is shared by my companion on this floating adventure.

'I've always said that clearing up rubbish, it's like picking scabs. It's disgusting but addictive – and I don't know why, but we almost always pick up a traffic cone every time we go out on Planet Patrol. Well done! You have your first one. If you want, you can take it home.'

Later, I do exactly that and load it into my car with a sense of pride. It feels like a talisman, a permanent reminder of this day spent exploring and talking.

I am with Lizzie Carr. She is one of the UK's most accomplished standup paddleboarders and a fearsome environmental campaigner. She is the founder of Planet Patrol, a global movement with a simple mission: to clean up the planet. It aims to redefine what can be achieved through collective action and citizen science by placing power in the hands of the people to tackle environmental issues. Today we have picked up at least 30 bits of detritus blemishing the River Trent.

I can see by the sparkle in her dark eyes that Lizzie is passionate about what she does. She took up paddleboarding in 2015 and since then has set three records. In 2016 she became the first person in history to paddleboard England's waterways, spending 22 days on her own on a 644-kilometre journey and logging 2000 photos of plastic on her way. A year later, she went on to become the first woman to paddleboard solo across the English Channel, and then the first person to paddleboard the entire length of the Hudson River, dodging lightning strikes and thunderstorms on the way.

I have paddleboarded before but am in no way an expert. I started dabbling during a long hot summer of lockdown when we were allowed to exercise only within a small radius of our homes. I bought my own board to explore the river near where I live. I chose it not for its paddling efficiency or safety but for its aesthetics. I spent quite a lot of time searching for the prettiest one I could find and waited an extra couple of weeks to make sure I got what I wanted. I loved its cheery eye-catching design: a white surface decorated with grey geometric shapes reminiscent of Māori art, and with sides and a bottom that are bright turquoise. You can't miss me!

I feel a bit embarrassed turning up with such a conspicuous board, but am delighted to see that the one Lizzie has chosen for our excursion is almost the same. Hers is about as wide as mine and she explains that it is easy to manoeuvre and keep her balance. On her long-distance challenges she would normally use a narrower, faster craft. I am glad she realises I am new to this.

The day started early for me, so that I could get across the country to Nottingham and we could begin by about 9.30.

Confused about our meeting place, I find myself driving down a one-way dirt track through flat green fields populated by bored looking sheep. When I negotiate a narrow, rickety bridge over a small tributary, the road starts to peter out and I come to a dead end. The way ahead is cut off by the deep water of the River Trent. I presume that I am lost.

With no mobile signal, I turn back to the nearest village to call Lizzie. It turns out I am not wrong; I am in the right place, and she is on her way but has been delayed by a sick baby. I wait in warm October sunshine opposite Shelford Church, a stunning, well-kept stone building that is the epitome of how an old English church should look: simultaneously imposing and welcoming.

Lizzie arrives and beckons me to follow her. She is being driven by her partner Russ, and when we get back to exactly where I came from, they tumble out of the van to give me a warm welcome. There's a shy smile from their one-year-old baby girl, who clings tightly to Lizzie's shoulder; I can see she is all bunged up with a sniffly cold.

One of the loveliest things about writing this book and meeting all the different women is that we meet in their safe space. Very often this has made it a family affair – and today is no exception. It is not unusual for Lizzie to take her daughter on her expeditions.

'I just love the fact she sees what we do and comes out in the morning, and you know, is part of all of this.'

I have always felt the same way with my own daughters. They have always been involved in what I do, seeing me both at work and on my triathlon adventures. In fact, one of the reasons I returned to sport so late in life was reading research showing that girls were far more likely to continue doing sport beyond their early years if they saw their own mothers exercising.

It feels like a real treat to have Russ there to help us too. He expertly helps me unfold my board, checks my paddle, and uses an electric compressor attached to the van's engine to inflate our boards. I don't have such a luxury and am used to huffing and puffing, using all my strength and breath for a manual pump. He has us both ready to go in just a couple of minutes.

Lizzie tells me that Russ has been her anchor. 'Sometimes I am so busy I can't think about anything other than what I am doing, and I just need someone to kind of help remind me about all the other things that exist around me.'

The forecast today is miserable, an 80 per cent chance of rain and high winds, so I squeeze myself into the thickest wetsuit I have; I don't trust myself not to fall in. In contrast Lizzie is wearing leggings, a fleece and a Gore-Tex jacket. We are both sporting colourful woolly bobble hats. Despite the inauspicious forecast, the sun comes out, reflecting off the smooth surface of the river. It is the colour of mud and reminds me of molten milk chocolate. It is sliding past us torpidly, as if in no hurry to get to the sea. I feel calmed by watching how slowly it is winding its way through the countryside, hugged on either side by high sandy banks.

Lizzie doesn't need to persuade me to wear a buoyancy aid. I am a confident swimmer but very aware of the dangers of moving water, and have tumbled off my board into the River Dee several times before. It always seems to happen when I least expect it and for no reason at all. I fasten my lifejacket tightly over my wetsuit, pull my hat over my head, and I am river ready!

I copy Lizzie as she clips her safety leash to a belt on her waist, then carefully lowers her board onto the water and climbs onto it. Our slow progress is being watched sceptically by a fisherman half disguised by green camouflage on the opposite bank. A raft of ducks floats past us. Lizzie has chosen a calm, secluded spot where we can push our boards gently and safely into the faster flow in the middle. I mirror her movements as best I can and, like her, kneel first to get my balance.

'Careful, careful, careful!' she says as I try to stand up where there are lots of large boulders perilously close to the surface. 'You can get your fin caught on the rocks and that's when you can jolt and fall off.'

When I am a safe distance from the bank and out of danger, I follow her calm instructions and gingerly stand up, one leg at a time. I might have done a small amount of paddleboarding, but no one has actually taught me what to do, or how best to do it, so I listen carefully to Lizzie, who has the patience of an experienced teacher.

She tells me how best to balance with my feet placed wide apart on the board, and to hold my paddle with a slight bend in my elbow. I laugh when she tells me that when she is instructing a group it is always the alpha males who don't pay attention and whizz off under their own steam. Invariably they fall in because they don't listen to her instructions, approach the banks at high speed, hit them with the tip of the board, come to a very sudden stop, and topple backwards into the water. The image tickles my sense of humour and reminds me to listen.

We are going to take a meandering route through gently rolling fields and farmland. Heading east away from the picturesque village of Stoke Bardolph we are aiming to reach Gunthorpe, about 6 kilometres downstream. It is a route popular with walkers, and a couple who are out with their springer spaniel are keeping us company, walking at the same speed as we float. I watch their dog bounding joyfully through the lush green grass.

Paddleboarding has not always been Lizzie's passion. It was a sport she discovered almost by accident, as the result of a life-changing medical diagnosis.

Growing up she had always liked nature, being outside and having adventures. During her early twenties, while she was working for a creative agency in London and climbing the corporate ladder, she tried to stay active. She would run a bit, climb, snowboard – and take nice holidays. Life seemed good, but she had a constant sense of foreboding. So much so that she decided to take some time out and travel.

Three months after her return, and at the age of only 26, she was diagnosed with thyroid cancer. The news changed the direction of her life.

'When you're faced with death, the reasons you want to live suddenly become overwhelmingly clear – and that is what you fight for. Lying in my hospital bed after my operation to remove the tumour, I could visualise the life I wanted and a clear sense of direction that I'd never experienced before. I just needed a second chance to follow through with it.'

When she first started treatment, Lizzie initially lived with her mother in Surrey, but because her mum is a foster carer she couldn't stay at home in the weeks after radiotherapy.

'I couldn't go back there because for about 10 days after treatment, I was still radioactive, and my levels were too high to be near children basically.'

Her alternative was to go and live with her dad on the Isles of Scilly.

'It was literally the best thing I did. It's the most peaceful, calming place and was a beautiful environment to be in. I would sit on the beach most afternoons, watching the world go by.'

It was while sitting chatting with her dad on a sunny day on the beach that she first saw someone paddleboarding. Right away, she wanted to try it.

'My dad told me I was bonkers, but I just felt that it looked like everything I needed was right there in front of me. So, I went over to the sailing club and asked if I could borrow a board. They asked if I had ever done it before. I said no, so I was surprised that they let me use it. I am so glad they did, it was like everything just clicked for me in that moment. It made me feel I was back to being me again, and that I could be out doing physical things.'

Paddleboarding became a crucial part of her recovery. She used it as a gentle, meditative way to get stronger and do physical exercise without overexerting herself.

'The best thing I think about paddling is you pick what you do and how you do it. If I wanted to be sitting down for this river right now, I could. If I wanted to take it lazily and slowly, I could. It is your choice how you manage your time on the water. For me everything just clicked. I'd never really had that before. I loved being active in sports but had never found a sport that I loved.'

Mirroring her words about taking it easy, we are no longer standing but sitting down, legs crossed in front of us as if at the beginning of a yoga class. I spot a cormorant ahead and see its distinctive S-shaped body disappear as it dives under the water in search of a fish. I count the seconds until it comes up again, scanning the surface to find it. To my surprise it pops up right beside Lizzie, and flicking its emerald green eye, gets a good look at the pair of us before it slips silently beneath her board.

It feels life-affirming, calming and tranquil to be floating peacefully downstream. Our conversation meanders lazily like the river, taking different turns, from discussing the joys of motherhood to the meaning of life. Our train of thought is stopped, though, when we are distracted by the unsightly view of litter, clustered in the reeds and branches on the lefthand bank of the river.

Drawn by the sight of ugly plastic bits and pieces clogging up the vegetation, we use our paddles to steer ourselves over to the edge. I manoeuvre myself carefully and lean over to grasp a milk carton with the pincers at the end of a long litter-picker. I drop it with a satisfying thump into a bright blue plastic bucket perched in front of Lizzie, with Planet Patrol written in large letters on the side.

Before I set out today on my floating adventure with Lizzie, I didn't think for a moment that she would turn me into an avid rubbish collector. But, to my great surprise, I discover that picking plastic out of the river is addictive: as soon as you grab one piece, your eye is drawn to another and another, you can't stop. It is, as Lizzie says, hard to unsee it.

We find crisp packets, bottles, bits of plastic bags and disintegrating cans. Those are just the big pieces, but there are also tiny particles. Those particles worry Lizzie more than the large pieces of rubbish we are plonking into the bucket. She worries about the birds and fish eating them and the impact it will have.

I ask her if what we are doing will make any difference.

'I really think it does. The way I see it is that everything's a victory, isn't it? Every single piece that you remove from nature is making a difference.'

So how did Lizzie go from that first day out on a beach on the Isles of Scilly to becoming a ground-breaking environmental campaigner?

Slowly. 'I was using nature and paddleboarding as a way of restoring my health and making me feel better. I ended up feeling like I wanted to give something back to the place that had looked after me. I chose the waterways because if I did it, I knew it would be a first, and I thought no one is really interested in rivers and canals. No one really looks at them and thinks that is an amazing place to go and have an adventure.'

It was during that first record-setting attempt to paddle the length of England's waterways that she found her purpose in life. Just like we have today, she noticed the rubbish strewn along the riverbanks.

'Some of the rivers were horrendous in terms of litter and pollution. I saw some appalling sights and started to realise how it was impacting wildlife around the river. The first thing I remember was seeing a coot's nest made of plastic, and that really shocked me. There were swans chewing on wrappers, plastic bags would get stuck on the back of my fin, bottles would roll under the board and pop out the other end. I started to think, *How can I show people what I am seeing, and what can I do to change it?* I started photographing it and logging it, and after that it just snowballed.'

That's an understatement. By the time I am paddling with Lizzie, 40,000 people in 113 different countries have taken part in a Planet Patrol clean-up. Over 460,000 examples of litter pollution have been uploaded in the Planet Patrol app. Those numbers increase daily. From talking to her, I realise the scale of what she is trying to do is enormous. I ask her if she really thinks she and all her Planet Patrollers can change things for the better.

'I think I am optimistic and hopeful. As an activist you have to be, because you have to believe in what you are trying to change. My ultimate goal for Planet Patrol is that people in power, policy makers, recognise what we are doing, that citizen science is a valid and credible approach to solving environmental issues. Between us we can gather a massive amount information far beyond what organisations are able to, and I want them to realise how powerful individuals can be in gathering data that can inform decisions.'

When we reach our destination, the inviting sight of a pub in Gunthorpe, we carefully clamber off our boards onto a rickety wooden jetty. It is higher above the water than we are, and I hold my breath as I wobble precariously, but steady myself, determined not to fall in and get wet and cold after having managed to stay dry all day. When we drag ourselves out successfully, we unload our haul of plastic with a thud onto the boards, like proud fishermen with the catch of the day.

I know that from now on, I will always be a rubbish collector. I want to believe – and indeed hope – that because of what she and others are doing, Lizzie's daughter won't have to be filling up buckets with plastic when she is her mother's age.

Months later, when I am practising freediving in pristine aquamarine waters off the coast of Sicily, I catch sight of a piece of white plastic strapping floating ghostlike above the seabed. As I dive down to remove it, I remember Lizzie and her mission to clean up the planet, one piece of rubbish at time – and realise she has changed me forever.

# 15

# Anoushé Husain
## *Indoor Climbing*
### North London

When I am on the wall nothing else exists but
me and my breath; there is no judgement.


I am not sure I have met someone as dynamic, determined, down
to earth, confident and courageous as paraclimber Anoushé
Husain, and I am struck by her ability to make others feel
empowered and brave.

We meet on a muggy day in September, one of those confusing
end-of-summer days when the season hasn't yet decided what
temperature it is going to be, and you don't know what to wear.
Manor House underground station is as far north as I have ever
travelled on the Piccadilly line and when I step out onto a busy
junction, all I know is that I am looking for a tower, a former
Victorian pump house that has been converted into a climbing
centre.

I am already jittery with nerves. I have never been climbing,
never been to a climbing wall, never even put my hand on a
climbing hold. Despite that, and somewhat bizarrely, I *am* the
owner of a pair of climbing shoes. I have them for an adventure
that got cancelled (COVID again), and they have now been

gathering dust at the back of a cupboard for a year and a half. I get them out, and they are tiny, and the sole is bent over and clawlike. I have tried them on, and although they are apparently perfect for my feet, they feel like they are half the size they should be. So tight, in fact, that they feel like an instrument of torture.

I don't have a clue what you are meant to wear for climbing but have chosen a pair of navy camo leggings and a bright orange, fluorescent top.

As I walk towards the climbing centre, anxious thoughts are tumbling through my head. *I don't know the basic rules! I don't understand the language. I don't know what the words mean. How do I tie the knots and make them safe? If I don't do it right, will I fall and hurt myself?* I feel ignorant, helpless.

Ahead of me, a dark tower dominates the apartments huddled beneath it. It looks like the kind of fortress that might trap Rapunzel, and from where in desperation she throws down her long hair. It must be 30 metres high, dark brick and skinny. It looks out of place, a castle that belongs in a horror story, not here beside a busy road, overlooking red double-decker buses.

We are meant to meet at 12, and the newsreader in me has prompted me to arrive a little early.

Inside is like the Tardis: massive. There are people and climbing walls everywhere. The walls are decorated with a kaleidoscope of plastic moulds scattered haphazardly. Climbers of all ages, shapes and sizes are dangling off overhangs, chatting, looking up, dusting chalk onto their hands, fixing harnesses. It is frenetically busy. I feel like I am in the way, another obstacle for climbers to manoeuvre around. A visually impaired woman is guided past me and makes her way to an iron stairway leading up inside the tower.

I feel dizzy as I watch a climber make her way up a wall high above me, right to the top, where she lets go and floats gently down in the safety of her harness. I can't work out whether it is too much coffee or the height making me feel funny and shaky. When I am nervous, my hands sweat, and I fear that could be a problem.

There is no sign of Anoushé.

I wait fidgeting, feeling out of place and conspicuous. I worry that I have travelled a long way on the wrong day. To play for time I fill out a registration form. It asks me all the usual mundane things – name, date of birth, emergency numbers – and then the killer question. *Do I accept that climbing is a dangerous sport and that it could cause serious injury or death?*

What have I let myself in for?

I hear Anoushé before I see her. Her distinctive lyrical voice carries across the cavernous reception, a potpourri of North London, French and American. She is a bundle of fizzing energy, grabbing things out of her wheelchair and chatting nine to the dozen to the receptionist.

She is not as tall as I thought and is dressed almost exactly the same as me – leggings, short sleeved T-shirt – with the addition of a light brown hijab. I see she is closely followed by a tall lean man wearing wraparound glasses. He is laden with harnesses and ropes and is obviously a climber as well.

'Hi, Louise! Welcome, lovely to see you. This is Ken.'

I remember that Ken is her husband. Later she tells me they first fell for each other when he gave her a lift back to London from Sheffield after a paraclimbing competition. Their journey home should have been a short one but became epically long because they had to drive through the middle of the brutal storm of February 2018, the Beast from the East. During those dark and slightly terrifying hours in the car, they got to know each other. They are a tight team, and often climb together.

Before I know it, I am buoyed up by their enthusiasm and swept along in the wake of Anoushé, who is pushing her super-sleek wheelchair, called Rose, to the bottom of a climbing wall.

For ages I have wanted to meet Anoushé, a one-woman dynamo. She is a British Muslim of Pakistani heritage working as a civil servant. Born missing her right arm below the elbow, she also has a complicated plethora of health conditions. These include Ehlers-Danlos syndrome, a connective tissue disorder which means, in simple terms, that her joints are too flexible and frequently dislocate. If that wasn't enough to deal with, she was diagnosed with cancer at the age of 23.

And I am here today because she is an accomplished sportswoman and a multi-award-winning campaigner. Her mission in life is to challenge misconceptions around disability and religion, and she does that largely through climbing.

I am here so she can teach me some of her trade.

Anoushé is straight-forward with a no-nonsense attitude. She barks orders at Ken: 'Grab your shoes and get your harness out.'

He does exactly what she says, giving as good as he gets in backchat. The two of them have a wonderful, positive, infectious energy.

She looks up at the wall rearing up beside us and I can see she is reading it like a book. 'I am looking for a nice route for you, one with nice easy jugs on.'

'Jugs?'

'Yes, like a large handle, one shaped like a jug that you just put your hand in. You don't have to grab it.'

Already I am learning a new language. She explains that the colours of the holds on the wall show you how difficult the route is. Normally you climb a single colour route, but she says I will be able to use a rainbow route. Any colour I like because I am a novice. *Thank goodness*, I think. *Anything to make it easier.*

It seems I will be going straight up the wall, no messing about or making a plan. I squeeze my feet into my shoes as

Anoushé commandeers Ken's harness. Between them they instruct me on how to get my legs in the right place, wiggle the belt over my hips and cinch it up supertight. I am getting more nervous by the minute.

I look at her shoes and see they are even smaller than mine. She says they hurt her feet, which swell up after a long session, but that is part of climbing.

'We are not going to send you up to the top, in case you have a panic attack up there. You are just going to get up a bit, get used to sitting back in your harness and then get back down again, and tell us how you feel.'

Anoushé had her first experience of climbing just before she was eight at school in Luxembourg. At the time she was doing lots of competitive swimming and a form of karate called Shotokan. She liked it enough to ask her parents if she could take it up as a hobby, but they worried it was too dangerous a sport and refused to let her pursue it.

She discovered a passion for it only years later, when she had moved to London and was recovering from cancer. A friend suggested that climbing might help her return to her previous strength.

At the time, she had all sorts of concerns. 'I won't be able to do my harness, I don't know how to tie my knots, I have changed body shape, the harness is going to highlight those things I am not comfortable with – and how am I going to do it with a headscarf?'

Her friend was having none of it, telling her she was making up excuses because she was scared. 'What is the worst that can happen? You don't like it, and you go and try another sport. What is the best? That you find something that changes your life.'

Her first session was painful, and she couldn't get to the top, her toes hurt, *everything* hurt – but she had a breakthrough. 'There were seconds in that time when I was so focussed on trying to find the right movement, trying to balance, that I forgot I was ill, I forgot the stuff I had been going through. For the first time in a very long time I felt normal, a human, a climber! It was an amazing form of escapism.'

From there she made swift progress, building up her strength in the gym and returning to the wall repeatedly over the next few months and making huge improvements. When she heard there were paraclimbing competitions to enter, she was so excited that she found a coach. And less than a year later, she was second in the UK in her category. This was at the same time that she was still struggling to walk from the Tube station to the climbing centre, exhausted by the effort of putting one foot in front of the other.

I met up with her six years into her climbing career and she is utterly professional. I am entranced by her nimble dexterity as I watch her use her left hand balanced against her right elbow to tie the safety knot that will connect me to the rope.

It is obvious this is second nature to her, a muscle memory, but she is also brilliant at explaining carefully how to make a figure of eight in the rope, double it so it can't come undone, and then how to check that it is safe and secure. This is a stopper knot – another term that I didn't know but which makes perfect sense. It will stop me if I fall.

I am much taller than her – 1.70 metres (5' 7") to her 1.50 metres (5') – and I presume much heavier. Even so, it is Anoushé who will be looking after me from her wheelchair on the ground. She is going to belay me, which by now I have worked out means she is going to control the rope attached to me, and keep it tight, so if I should happen to fall, I won't fall far.

Together she and Ken work like a crack team of disciplined coaches.

'Right, Louise, you can climb up using any colour. Just use what is comfortable, go as high as those two circles, then let your hands go. Sit down as if you are on a dining chair, keep your legs straight, feet on the wall. I will lower you down.'

Impelled by their enthusiasm, I just get on with it and, to my surprise, manage to clamber halfway up the wall before they tell me it is time to sit back and come down. I am sweaty, heart racing with the adrenaline, and want to go straight back up again.

'You are clearly fine with heights and taking instruction, or we would have a problem by now, so go to the top using only one colour!'

I worry that I will pull Anoushé out of her chair and hurt her if I fall. She tells me she is more than used to being yanked from her chair and assures me I am no problem at all.

I look up at where I am heading, and tell her it makes me feel dizzy. She tells me not to look so high. Instead, I focus on her voice and closely listen to her instructions, this time just using the black. I grip onto each hold for dear life. My breathing is heavy and my heart racing. But with Ken and Anoushé reassuring me, I make it all the way to the top. The adrenaline rush when I sit back in my harness and am gently lowered to the ground makes me shiver. My hands and forearms are sore, the muscles tired from using so much force. Anoushé laughs and tells me I have been working harder than I need to and gripping way too tight.

I get my breath back as Anoushé prepares to tackle the wall. I am too scared to have her life in my hands, so Ken is in charge of safety and is the one to belay her. She is astonishing to watch. She moves with effortless fluidity, using every part of her body to move upward – her left hand, the crook of her strong right elbow, her hips and her heels. She makes it look so easy, she seems to be moving horizontally not vertically. I gasp as she makes a leap of faith and jumps from one tricky hold to another, for a moment swinging in mid-air. She is absorbed in what she is doing. I can see it is not just a physical feat but a mental challenge too, to carefully plan her route.

Watching her move, I can see why she finds solace in her sport.

'The thing about the climbing wall is that unless they have reset a route, the climbing wall is practically going to be the same thing every time you go there. You go there angry, sad, frustrated or stressed and the wall hasn't changed, only you have. So, if your climbing has changed, that is a reflection of who you are on that day. It is like a non-judgemental mirror of your state of mind and body on the day. When I am on the wall, nothing else exists but me and my breath; there is no judgement.'

It is almost time for me to go and leave Anoushé to her session. I feel humbled, inspired and lucky to have been able to spend time with her. She has a very special gift, the ability to share her passion, passing it on and giving others a confidence in themselves.

Over the years she has won so many awards for her work around disability and sport, from the Asian Woman of Achievement Award to the Award for Inspiration at The Sunday Times Sportswomen of the Year Awards, but praise is not her motivation.

'Winning awards has been surreal, but the amazing imposter syndrome part of me says I don't see what special thing I am doing besides leading my life and sharing what I do. I go up, I climb, I climb a bit hard, I go home, and I share what I do. I am sharing my truth. When I had cancer, I found it to be a hugely isolating experience, and if I can share and help someone feel less alone and get help and take a step for themselves, that's why I do it. So they don't feel the same sense of isolation.'

I ask her one final question. If she could have a choice what would her superpower be?

'Infinite strength. I keep dreaming of moves I need to be stronger for, and I don't have the strength yet. I keep having visualisations of me doing these moves, and I see them, and I see what I can do if I were strong enough. I want super-strength for those really hard-ass moves.'

A few months after we meet, I see that she has been using some of those hard-ass moves to set a new female Guinness World Record for the greatest vertical distance climbed one-handed on a climbing wall. She smashed it. The previous record was 200 metres and she climbed 375.85 metres. In practical terms that meant she went up and down the wall we tackled 51 times in a row!

Her achievement reflects a motto she lives by: *Keep believing in your impossible.*

# 16

# **Rhiane Fatinikun**
## *Hiking*
## The Peak District, Derbyshire

Are you going to be walking in those?

It is a beautiful spring day. I am standing on a ridge with a staggering 360-degree view over hills blanketed in the subtle, purple-pink hues of the deep lush heather growing riotously across the moorland. The steep grassy slopes falling away are decorated by sheep so perfectly white and fluffy I can hardly believe they are real. It looks like they have been carefully placed there as part of a delicately created model of the British countryside. The sky is an impossibly pale blue and cirrus clouds are streaking high in the haze, criss-crossed by vapour trails from aeroplanes long departed. The beauty makes me breathless.

My companion on this day is locked in concentration, focussed on an Ordnance Survey app on her phone and in deep discussion with two walkers who have asked for help. I know why they have chosen to ask her for information; she looks like she knows exactly what she is doing. She is at home here high on the hill, at one with the countryside. She looks like a leader that others would willingly follow. It has always been like this for her.

'I've always been a leader. I was a leader at school. Did all the sports teams, all that kind of thing. I suppose I have always had that kind of personality.'

The first thought that went through my head when I saw Rhiane Fatinikun, waiting patiently for me on the kerb in a deserted Edale Car Park in the depths of the High Peak in Derbyshire, was that she is dressed perfectly for our outing. Yellow and green off-road trainers, thick socks pulled over the bottom of her black Sweaty Betty leggings, black T-shirt, red fleece jacket, a compact rucksack on her back, and a very stylish pair of sunglasses. I particularly love her immaculately manicured nails: pink with a red tip.

I catch her look me up and down, and as she looks at my shoes, I see a flash of consternation. She says tentatively, 'Are you going to be walking in those?'

I laugh. They are Doc Martins, great on a high street but not made for hiking. 'No, don't worry, I have walking boots in the car!'

I see the relief on her face. It is only later that she tells me she has led hiking groups for women who have turned up to walk in high-heeled trainers or sliders.

We are not alone today; I have my two dogs Ruby and Waffle in tow.

Rhiane's passion for hiking is infectious. Her mission in life is to challenge stereotypes and the lack of representation of the Black community in the outdoors – and she is making a massive difference. Back in 2019, she set up the organisation Black Girls Hike (BGH), which now has members across the country, from Manchester to Bristol, Coventry, Milton Keynes, Devon, Dorset and Nottingham.

As we set off up the hillside towards Mam Tor, the first summit on our circuitous walk, we negotiate our way carefully over a rickety wooden stile with a sign above it asking people to keep dogs on a short lead from 1 March. We both assume this is due to the lambing season but read that it is actually to protect ground-nesting birds. Either way, I put the dogs on a lead as a lone sheep with a black face and shaggy white coat observes us intently from the other side of the fence. Rhiane immediately adopts Waffle, my golden Labrador, and the two of them stride ahead purposefully in front of me. Rhiane talks as fast as she walks, hardly drawing breath. At school her teachers would ask: 'Have you got gills? You hardly need to breathe when you speak!'

The musicality and rhythm of her voice is accompanied by the percussion of my walking poles clicking on the flinty stones. I listen intently as she explains she set up BGH almost on a whim.

'It all started here in the Peak District, right where we are. I was thinking about ways to do something more worthwhile. I had a really unfulfilling job at the time, and I was also experiencing anxiety, which meant I was always panicking about how I was spending my time. I was on a train going through the Peak District and I was watching groups of older people, getting on and off the train and I was, like, that is what I am going to do: I am going to take up hiking. It is on my doorstep; I am on the train right now and I could literally just get off and do it.'

The only hike she had ever been on before that day was with her aunt, who once took her for a walk in Bolton, but just like that, she decided to become a hiker.

Straight after that train journey, Rhiane set up an Instagram page, calling it Black Girls Hike (BGH) right from the start. She chose a walk from the *Manchester Evening News*, advertised online that she was going to do it and asked people to join her. It struck a chord and almost immediately she started getting messages.

She was unprepared – for both the walk and the impact she was going to have. 'I had none of the kit. Two days before the hike I bought a waterproof and a pair of walking boots from Sports Direct. I didn't even wear in my walking boots; the first time I ever wore them was on the way to the hike. I remember being surprised to see so many people turn up, especially some that were already hikers. BGH is about challenging stereotypes, one that I was guilty of holding myself: that Black people didn't hike. I didn't have time to go and practise that route – and I was an hour late for the first walk because I had to wait for my sister to give me a lift! When I got there, there were 14 people waiting, and I was like, *Oh my God!* I didn't even think people were going to turn up. Not only that, we had a journalist there from *The Voice* on my very first hike and she put us on the front page!'

That walk in Hollingworth Lake in Littleborough, Greater Manchester, changed Rhiane's life. 'Everyone enjoyed the hike and they wanted to come again, and we started getting messages from all over the country about hikes.'

Just as she is telling me that story of how it all began, far away in the distance, I hear the unmistakable sound of metal wheels scraping along a railway track. It's a moment of surreal serendipity. As we turn around and look back over the vast valley towards Edale, we spot below us two jaunty blue and white carriages of a train chugging along the Hope Valley Line, from Sheffield to Manchester – the very train where she had been sitting daydreaming about a different life. Gliding through the countryside, slipping past grey stone houses, it looks like a model train on a model railway.

I am not super fit right now, and am breathless from the gradient, but we have made great progress, and reached a ridge that leads steeply uphill along a painstakingly and delicately laid, sand-coloured flagstone path. The wide track snakes before us, wandering over the rolling hills. High above us, taking advantage of the breeze, are three paragliders, their brightly coloured fabric wings floating silently on the thermals. It is peaceful and ethereal.

This is a Tuesday afternoon, and I say to Rhiane that I feel a bit naughty, self-indulgent, as if I have bunked off school. She laughs and says she knows how I feel, and how blessed and lucky she is that this is, in fact, her office.

It hasn't always been easy, though. After appearing on the BBC's *Countryfile* programme, which celebrates all things about the British countryside, Rhiane tells me she was viciously trolled.

'You get all these people who say they love the outdoors, but if you love it so much why wouldn't you share it? Why wouldn't you want someone else to enjoy it?'

Her first walk in London was a testing experience too. 'It was in August 2020, and we went to Epping Forest around the time of the Black Lives Matter protests, and over 100 people turned up. It was insane! But some people don't know how to avert their gaze, literally they were looking at us like this . . .'

She stops in her tracks and turns round to stare at me intently. Her glare feels aggressive and intimidating.

'And they were saying, "What is going on? What is going on?!" There were people asking, "What is this? Is this a protest?" Because they assume that so many Black people together is a protest. Some people say Black joy is a protest, it is resistance, right? Because people don't want you to feel joy.'

I ask her how she hopes to change people's perceptions. From her point of view, my question needs to be turned upside down.

'You need to focus on the people whose perception *can* change. We are on such a mission, and it is so meaningful, impactful and beneficial for our community – those are the type of people we should be trying to engage with, not people who don't want to change.'

It doesn't feel like very long before we reach the summit of Mam Tor, where we stop for a few minutes, both leaning our elbows on the top of the stone trig point, smiling happily for a photo in the sunshine.

As we carry on along the Great Ridge, taking in the views for miles on both sides, our conversation is briefly interrupted as Rhiane helps the lost walkers. When she has sent them safely on their way, we make our way to Hollins Cross, an ancient crossroads and the lowest point on the ridge. Many years ago, before the roads were built, it was the route for packhorses carrying goods on their way between Edale and Castleton.

I look upwards towards the steep path, which has high uneven steps, and wonder whether my dodgy knee is going to be OK on the tricky terrain. Despite my doubts, we decide together to take the hard path, and are rewarded by the collection of waist-high cairns scattered across the top. They look extraordinary, out of place, as if a group of diminutive aliens had landed there from another planet. We pour over the sundial which marks the summit, Lose Hill, and try to work out what we can see, and if we can discern the famous contours of Kinder Scout to our left. It is hard to make the letters out: the place names etched into the bronze disc have been worn down over the years by so many hands touching them.

I ask Rhiane what changes she sees in the many people she has helped introduce to the countryside.

'I see a shift in them, it is like an awakening. We are a group that is all about taking up space in an unapologetic way. I would like that, when people leave the group, they can be that way anywhere. I want to give them confidence, so even when they are the only Black person in a space, they don't have to be like a wallflower; they can be themselves.'

Rhiane has ambitious plans for Black Girls Hike. It is no longer just about hiking. There have been groups kayaking, caving, canoeing and climbing, and BGH is now a training provider delivering navigation courses.

'What we are doing now is getting all our leaders trained up so we can have more outdoor leaders. It is really important to have Black outdoor leaders because representation is important, not just for our community but other communities as well. It is really important that you see Black people in responsible roles, and senior roles so that everyone can have something to aspire to and that people who are not from our community can learn to respect those leaders.'

What is her ultimate ambition?

'I want to be able to move past conversations about how to diversify the outdoors, and just have an outdoors that is actually genuinely inclusive and diverse. I want to remove all of the barriers to participation and just see our community thriving in nature.'

She is indefatigable and her determination is infectious. I have no doubt that she will keep pushing Black Girls Hike, and that she will continue to change lives. Thanks to her, others will go out and enjoy our beautiful countryside as we have today.

# 17

# Susie Chan
## *Ultrarunning*
## Thorney Island, West Sussex

Running is a roller coaster, no two days are the same. Some days … I think I am flying. Other days I think, *Why is this so hard?*

When I set out to write this book, I assumed a large part of it would be about running. There are so many runners out there who I wanted to meet, as well as some adventures that I wanted to attempt. It was not to be, though; injury intervened. The deterioration of my knee and subsequent operation meant that in the year of writing and researching I have hardly run at all, but I was determined to get at least one run in the book and asked a fabulously fearless runner to accompany me.

Susie Chan is a huge inspiration to me – and I am not alone.

There is a picture of her hurtling down a giant sand dune in Morocco during the Marathon des Sables, one of the toughest multi-day endurance races on the planet. It is one of the most dynamic and inspiring photographs I have ever seen. Dressed in black shorts and white T-shirt, with a rucksack on her back laden with water bottles and a sleeping-mat, she is going full pelt. Sand is flying from her feet, and her dark brown hair, tied in a high ponytail, is streaming out behind her. She wears a pair of Aviator sunglasses, a black and white sun visor and, most striking of all, a huge smile on her face. You can recognise when someone is doing the thing they love, and for me the photograph is a moment in time which captures what that brings: focus, strength and freedom.

I love her story too: a fabulously encouraging example of zero to hero, which will resonate with runners, non-runners or reluctant runners like me. It couldn't be more fitting that she is the runner included in this book.

Eleven years ago, Susie was a single mum, often sitting on the sofa with a cigarette, watching hospital dramas like *Holby City* while drinking a bottle of wine. Over a decade later, her life could not be more different.

She has completed all six of the World Marathon Majors, the largest and most renowned marathons in the calendar: Tokyo, Boston, London, Berlin, Chicago and New York. At the time of writing, she has finished the gruelling Marathon des Sables more times than any British female and has run five 100-mile (160-kilometre) races.

She brushes it off lightly, but I have to mention that she has completed many of those races after being diagnosed with thyroid cancer.

When I meet her, she is deep into endurance training for another huge challenge. She is trying to qualify for one of the toughest races in the world: the Badwater Ultramarathon, in America's Death Valley. Not only do you have to run a 100-mile (160-kilometre) race to qualify, but the race guards its prestigious reputation by being invitation only. Your entry must be approved by a board, which will decide whether you are worthy of a place or not. Susie describes it as the pinnacle of endurance running. I can't imagine they will turn her down, but she is not betting on her chances.

After over a year of trying to run with her, and having to cancel as the extent of my knee problems slowly revealed themselves, we meet in a tiny car park on the south coast, next to Thorney Island. It is early in the day, and apart from the owner of a tiny blue and white coffee van who is setting up her stall for the morning's trade in caffeine and cakes, we are the only ones there.

The idea is that we will go for a run/walk of 5 miles (8 kilometres) or so. I am still at the start of my rehabilitation and my physio has said I could probably manage 3 miles (5 kilometres). So I am already, as usual, pushing it a bit!

We set off under dark clouds across a scrubby field. A grey horse, which is grazing absent-mindedly, watches out of the corner of its eye as we pick our way over tussocks. Susie tells me to set the pace, to run when I want and walk when I want, and we start off at a steady jog. We navigate through a marina and on to the top of a grassy sea defence with the hazy sight of Hayling Island to our right and soggy marshland on our left, which must be a birdwatcher's paradise.

I ask where her passion for running started.

'Eleven years ago, my younger brother signed me up to a half marathon. At the time my evenings were a bottle of wine, watching telly. I didn't do anything, I smoked, I was very unfit, very unhealthy. It wasn't a good lifestyle. I was in my mid-thirties and I had my daughter, and I was conscious I wanted to be a better role model to her, but I wasn't sure how I was going to do that.

'When he signed me up to the half marathon, I didn't really know how far a half marathon was. I didn't know anything, not a clue. I started training by running to the big Tesco near me and back to my house. My longest run I think might have been 9 miles [14 kilometres].

'Race day came and my brother picked me up and I said, "I am not going!" Somehow, he persuaded me to get in the car and we ended up in this field. It was terrifying and another runner said, "Do you like trails?" I said, "I don't know, what do you mean?" I had no idea the whole thing was off-road, up and down hills, over sand, over stiles. On reflection, a quite difficult, lumpy run. But you know what it's like if you don't know anything different. It was my first ever race, so I had no clue. I did it, died quietly but finished, and I couldn't believe I had run 13 miles [almost 21 kilometres]. I did it in about two hours, 17 minutes, which was actually not bad for a tricky trail run.'

I have to interrupt, because from my point of view two hours, 17 minutes for that kind of off-road, hilly run is more than *not bad*, it is *very respectable*.

During that first half marathon, Susie had a life-changing, eureka moment.

'I was around 9 miles [14 kilometres] in, and I realised all I needed to do was just keep going. The finish was within my grasp. That was my turning point. I switched from a feeling of fear to *I can do this*. I was suddenly not scared any more of failing. It was incredible. I genuinely loved it.

'That was my turning point. I don't think there is anything like that first finish, is there? It is so empowering to have fear be turned into confidence. Realising I have done it; I have actually done it. It was the first step for me on a massive ladder of confidence-building. Of *what can I do next?*'

I love the irony in her voice when she says, 'It escalated quite quickly from there!'

That is putting it lightly! Straight after, Susie signed up for a 10k as well as another half marathon.

'I went all-in. I joined a running club. That was a big game changer; I found that very enabling. I was terrified the first time I went. They were a really lovely running club, a local one, not very competitive. They opened my eyes to trails, as that is where they ran. I would be running around gorgeous paths thinking, *This is just beautiful. This is my town. This is where I live* – and I never knew because I had been sitting at home drinking wine, driving to the shops and back without realising there were all these places 3 miles [5 kilometres] from my house. It blew open this whole world out there of running, and I went on this journey of discovery.'

It is an extraordinary journey.

Clearly, she fell in love with running on that first race, and found her passion in life, her raison d'être. I am interested to find out when she knew she was good at it. Before she even answers my question, I guess that she will say she isn't.

'In the grand scheme of running, I am very much a middle packer, and I am very comfortable being there. I enjoy it. What I am good at, and I know I am good at this, is if I have decided to do something, I will do it, and I will do everything in my power to do it. In those difficult environment races, like a 100 miler, I will do everything in my power to get to the finish line. Mentally I am very good, my legs just aren't that fast. Some people have got speed and I just plateau at a certain speed – and that is me and I am alright with that.'

Good is a relative value. Her fastest marathon time is, for me, an unimaginable three hours, 23 minutes!

I am a bit out of breath now and relieved when our progress is abruptly halted by an intimidating, 3 metre/10 foot-high, chain-link fence topped with barbed wire. Susie explains that the land ahead of us is owned by the Ministry of Defence, and it looks suitably well protected. There are signs warning that CCTV cameras are watching us, and that they are monitored 24 hours a day. A massive red notice announces in large capital letters 'CRITICAL INFORMATION', and includes a warning about strong currents in the water and the possibility of finding asbestos on the foreshore. I don't need any more encouragement to do exactly as it says and 'stay on the coastal path at all times'.

Susie presses the metal buzzer, and as we wait for someone to respond, I catch my breath. After six long resonant beeps that merge with the cry of the gulls overhead, there is a metallic click, and the access gate opens. I am spooked by the thought that there is someone in a guardroom remotely deciding we can be let in.

We set off running again, but as soon as the ground gets uneven or pebbly, I have to slow down to a walk as I scrunch the stones under my shoes. I am like an ungainly puppy compared to Susie, who is as sure-footed, as elegant and as fast, as a gazelle.

Watching Susie run is fascinating: she looks like a feather floating across the ground. It doesn't seem to matter if there is tufty grass, shingle or sand under her feet; every springy stride is the same.

She is a Peloton running instructor, and I ask her what she tells people to help them run well.

'Relax the shoulders, make sure your arms are relaxed. Stand tall. Imagine you have a helium balloon on a thread attached to the top of your head holding it up. You need to have a lightness to you.'

I do as she says and immediately feel better. I tell her that she makes it look effortlessly easy, but she assures me it is not.

'Running is a roller coaster, no two days are the same. Some days – they are few and far between – I think I am flying. Wow. Other days I think, *Why is this so hard?* Everybody has that, don't they?'

I am taken aback. I had assumed that such a successful runner as Susie would never think it is hard. It is reassuring to hear her say that she has the same negative thoughts as I do.

'Everyone has days when it is awful. Not every run is a good run. Not everything can be excellent. Life isn't like that. With running, you have to take the rough with the smooth and there are going to be more average days than great days, more average days than rubbish days. So you have to bank those days where you are flying and bank the bad ones too because you still did it. In fact, I think the bad days count for more because you've still gone and done it.'

That's the reason Susie posts every run she ever does: good runs, bad runs, slow runs, fast runs. To show runners who are struggling, she puts every single one on Strava for everyone to see. This run, she tells me, will go up too.

We have to slow down again. Not because I am out of breath, but because a herd of inquisitive calves are wandering along the narrow path along the top of the flood protection bank. Most are black, one is the colour of a chocolate brownie, and all have yellow tags with their numbers punched into their ears. I can see their mothers on our left and there is a precarious sharp drop onto a shale beach littered with slippery brown seaweed on the right. That option looks treacherous underfoot. We are both reluctant to get between the calves and the rest of the herd, so we wait until they slowly move out of the way.

When we get past them, we look back to see them staring at us quizzically, and take a photo. I am glad we turned around, as we can see the beginnings of a brighter day. The clouds have gone, and pale blue skies are mirrored in the glassy, still water.

I ask her about her toughest races and how she gets through them. I am surprised when she says that one of the worst was a 10k. She was in such agony trying to hit the pace she wanted that she nearly stopped half a mile in.

'It is astonishing what the body can do when the mind is on side. When it isn't, it is awful. It was only a 10k, but I just thought: *I might have to stop now – what is the point?* I was having this mental battle with myself. It was all on me. You put these pressures on yourself. I had chosen to make myself miserable, as I wasn't running as fast as I would like.

'I have changed since then. Now I am of the mindset that you just do as best you can on that day. If I am not as fast as I would like to be, it doesn't need to ruin my day or ruin my week. It just is what it is.'

I look down at my watch and to my astonishment realise that, distracted by our chatter, I have run/walked 3¾ miles (6 kilometres). I can't believe I have managed to go so far; it is the furthest I have attempted to run in months, and my knee doesn't seem to hurt at all. The only part of me complaining is my hips.

Susie tells me that we have broken the back of the run, and I am relieved. I am loving it, but I am also glad to know it will be over soon.

'We are at the beach now, and then it is not too far from here. Maybe 2 miles [3.2 kilometres].'

Our conversation turns to the toughest race she has ever done. A multi-day jungle ultra in Peru, for which she admits she had underprepared. 'You had to be self-sufficient, and it was very wet, very muddy and treacherous. For some of the river crossings the water was up to my chest. On one of them I lost my footing and got swept about half a mile [800 metres] downstream. Once I got out of the river, I had to battle my way through the jungle with no path. It was scary. I had some very sketchy moments on my own in the middle of the Peruvian jungle. That was hard.'

I ask her if she wanted to quit the race.

'I wanted to give up, but I couldn't, as there was no one anywhere near me to hand over my race number to. I remember doing this primal scream at the top of a mountain. That night I told the race director, *I just can't do this. I am done.* He said: *Eat, sleep and see you how you feel.*'

You can imagine what she did! Yup, the next day she got up and carried on and finished the race. 'It was so mentally tough. But a lot of it was my own fault, as I had underprepared.'

I want to know how all these extraordinary experiences have changed Susie. There are the obvious lifestyle changes, but what about the way she feels about herself?

'This is really hard to say without sounding really cheesy. It has changed my life. It has changed who I am in a good way. I am a lot more confident. Eleven years ago in a meeting room of four to five people saying things, I wouldn't speak. I went under the radar, kept a low profile.

'I have discovered the extrovert within me. Running is part of it, and so is getting older and caring less about what people think. I am 47 and I have embraced my age. I feel proud of it. I would love older women to know that they can do what the hell they want; that they are capable of it; that the barriers that exist are finite; that they exist in your head.'

The sun is out now. We are running along a wide, elevated stone path, and on our left is a fast-flowing stream, which looks like a man-made channel to drain water from the marsh. Ahead of us is a fence.

'That's the gate and then we are going to see the car, and then there is that little van and we can have a coffee. Do you want a coffee?'

Absolutely, I did. 'What time is it?'

'11.57!'

'Shit, shall we run?' I ask optimistically. Then I do the calculations: we have three minutes until closing, and our only chance of getting a coffee is if Susie sprints to try and get there. In a flash she is off, like a 100-metre runner out of the blocks. There is no way I can keep up with her, she is on a mission. As she disappears into the distance, I shout after her: 'Any kind of coffee, please!'

I watch with a mixture of envy and admiration as she springs away from me, then get distracted by the sight of sailing boats taking advantage of the light breeze whipping up white horses on the water. I follow a small blue fishing boat making its way purposefully into the harbour. I don't realise I have lost sight of her until I come to a fork in the path, and start to worry that I didn't see which way she went.

After a few moments' thought, I figure that if I follow the water's edge along the low seawall I can't go wrong. The tide is in now and is so high that I can't walk on the foreshore. I'm pushed inland into a boatyard with dozens of sailing boats tethered like ponies in neat lines. I can see the path meandering parallel to the water's edge and think that must be the way Susie has gone.

But then to my consternation I notice that the tiny lifting bridge over the narrow canal is up. Its wooden boards are pointing vertically skywards to make way for a boat to come through. I judge from the way the three men are manoeuvring the mechanism that it is going to be impassable on foot for quite a while. I turn around and get increasingly anxious as I find myself in dead end after dead end, unable to find a way out.

I realise I am definitely heading in the right direction when I see the same grey horse which had watched us lazily as we set out. This time it looks up at me, its ears pricked forward with interest, just as Susie comes around the corner with a smile on her face and a coffee in each hand. The van owner had waited especially for us. I couldn't be more delighted, especially when Susie hands me half of a home-baked beetroot brownie.

We sit on a bench in warm sunshine, chatting and sipping our hot drinks. My body is trembling from the exertion. We talk about her job as a running coach for Peloton and how it has served to remind her of her running roots.

'I have spent so long running in this ultramarathon world where things are very normalised – like running a marathon as a training run. It's not normal, is it? And now in this job I get messages like *I have just run my first mile without stopping. I have run my first 5k. I am 65 and I have run my first two miles without stopping.* It is a nice leveller; you realise that running is for all. Because the ultrarunning world, as astonishing, incredible and inspiring as it is, is not normal, it is "extra" ordinary. It has been really great to reconnect with running and to be able to share this love of running with people who love running, all over the world.'

I ask for her advice for my running journey. My plan, though I hardly dare articulate it, is to run the London Marathon, which is six months away (and will be nine months after my operation). Given that I can only just do what we have done today –walk/run 10k – it feels like a monumental task.

'Recover, slow and steady, don't be a hero. I am not worried about your mindset, you can tough it out. You just need to get your fitness, which won't take very long. You commit to things so you will be fine.'

That is good advice, which I will take with me – to commit. Perhaps, for once, I will commit to recovery and working towards the marathon and try not to add any other extreme challenge in the meantime. Apart from her attempt to get to Badwater, what is her ultimate ambition as a runner?

'I really want to be like a 76-year-old lady who I often see at Park Run. She runs for the joy of being part of the community. I want to be able to take part forever, not have this thing that I love taken away from me.'

With that thought we part ways. Later she sends me her Strava map of our run. The shape is a perfect diamond. We couldn't have drawn it more accurately if we had tried. Like her many legions of fans, I feel encouraged by Susie – and hope that one day, just for a day, I too will feel like I am flying.

# And Finally

Wow, what a year it has been!

I set out on a mission to tell the stories of courageous women, and looking back over the extraordinary adventures we shared together has left me feeling overwhelmed, inspired and humbled.

I feel like I have been on a journey of my own. The challenges we have undertaken have been more epic than I could have imagined; they have taken me to places that I had not dreamed of and pushed me both physically and mentally. I have been up against the edge of my boundaries and surprised myself with what I am capable of. I have learned so much from every one of them: how to take on big challenges, how to dig deep in adversity and how to stay determined when the odds are against you.

Hearing about their experiences and achievements first-hand has left me even more frustrated than I was, that they and other women like them have not been celebrated as they deserve to be. Why? Because we can learn from them, relate to them and be inspired by them.

There are so many recurring and important themes that are knitted like golden threads through the stories in this book.

First up is their fearless bravery.

Their determination in the face of what might seem like intimidating and insurmountable challenges to carry on regardless, heads held high. Zee Alema, a Black Muslim woman who despite the culture of drinking in rugby kept turning up, kept playing. Mollie Hughes, who struggled to find sponsorship for her mountaineering expeditions but kept on asking. Caroline Bramwell, a triathlete with a serious health condition, who has failed twice to finish an Ironman race but is going to turn up at the start line until she has the medal around her neck. Their tenacity, and their determination to remain undaunted by adversity, is admirable.

I was humbled too by their collective modesty.

Something I noticed in every conversation I had is that all these women are relentlessly self-deprecating. Lucy Gossage makes light of being an Ironman Champion at the same time as saving lives. Kadeena Cox, whose cycling academy is clearing the pathways for others like her, describes it as 'making a difference in a small way'. Mimi Anderson calls herself a *bike-list* not a cyclist. Belinda Kirk brushes off her multiple expeditions and Guinness World Record. None of these women are asking for praise, for kudos, for accolades. They love what they do, it fulfils them, it is important to them. But wearing their achievements lightly is no reason for them to be disregarded, ignored, or undervalued.

At the start of the book, I mentioned that I believe in the adage *If you see it, you can be it*. Heroes and role models will ignite your imagination and open your eyes to new horizons. Without them, the world is a much poorer and much more limited place.

What I have witnessed over the last 12 months has reinforced this for me and demonstrated how important and how impactful heroes can be. They can change lives.

Mitali and Anaya Khanzode are a perfect example, standing next to a 10-year-old girl who had braved the swim from Alcatraz because of them. Kadeena Cox does the same. Her trailblazing academy has already opened the doors for one paracyclist world champion, and there will be others. Susie Chan was inspired to become an ultrarunner after seeing Mimi Anderson's achievements. Cath Pendleton's exploits in ice swimming are opening doors to the joys of open water to other women, inspired by her to get back in the water.

They may not all know it, but these women are changing other people's lives for the better. They are part of a powerful virtuous circle.

Thirty years ago, I wrote a dissertation for my degree, examining the damaging impact of discrimination against women in the media, in newspapers, radio and TV, and what it meant for their perceived value in society. The issue was much worse then, but it still exists. As a mother to two daughters, I see it and am incensed. It is subtle – as subtle as me not reading the first headline or doing the first interview – as subtle as only hearing from male heroes – but it is there and it needs to be changed.

So how can you make a difference? How can we change it?

Firstly, by choosing to read this book you are part of altering the narrative. You can pass on the stories to your friends, your colleagues, your family, your children, other people who will be inspired by these women.

Secondly, you can call out bias, unfairness or misrepresentation when you see it.

I will be forever grateful to the woman, a stranger, who came up to me at a charity lunch and asked, 'Why is it that the men presenting with you always get to start the programme?' I was aware of this already, but she made me sit up and take notice, gather the evidence, and do something.

Thirdly, you can amplify the voices of your heroes, of women like these. You can be the one to sing their praises, shout about their accomplishments, their triumphs and successes. Follow them on social media, tell their stories, pass their message on. We can do it for them. Together we can make a difference.

# Acknowledgements

Thank you first and foremost to the 18 incredible women in this book.

Thank you for responding with enthusiasm to my outlandish requests to meet you in the first place, which mostly came out of the blue on social media. Thank you for welcoming me into your worlds, sharing your precious time and your passions with me. You have all been incredibly generous, honest and open, and I have been changed by your stories for the better. I feel bonded to you all, as if we are now part of a feisty and fearless sisterhood.

Thank you to my most important team, David, Mia and Scarlett. Thank you for never being fazed by my madcap ideas and for supporting me as I pursue them. Thank you for the moments you remind me that I can achieve crazy things when I think I have bitten off more than I can chew, for the confidence and belief in myself that you give me. Thank you for being my safe haven to which I will always return. I love you all more than I can put into words.

Thank you to Matt Lowing at Bloomsbury for putting up with my rants about women's stories not being told and for letting me do exactly that here in this book. I am sorry I didn't make it into a space rocket, but maybe there is a next time!

Thank you to my literary agent Elly James at hhb for your patience, gentle cajoling, and reminders about deadlines. Without you I would not have finished these incredible journeys.

There are many more amazing women that I would have loved to have talked about, and I know everyone will have someone else they would like to have seen included. *That's* my point. There are hundreds of incredible women out there who have their own stories to tell and we can all be part of telling them.